# The Historical Development of the Martello Tower in The Channel Islands

by

*Eric Grimsley*

E. J. Grimsley

1

Published in Guernsey by
SARNIAN PUBLICATIONS,
Rousse, 23 Clos du Villocq, Castel, Guernsey.

ISBN 0-9513868-0-8

Designed and Produced by Go Guernsey Publications.
Printed by The Guernsey Press Co. Ltd.

# Abstract

by Rona Cole,
*Curator*

Candie Museum & Art Gallery,
Guernsey.

The Channel Islands, once part of the Duchy of Normandy, became linked to England in 1066 and, after King John's loss of Normandy in 1204, the Islands remained loyal to the Crown. It is not surprising, therefore, in view of their proximity to France, that these islands have so many fortifications. This book examines the 'Martello' towers in Guernsey and compares these towers with those in Jersey and England.

From among this assortment of towers, built at various stages of history, can be seen the development of the English Martello tower. The island's strategic position lent itself to the building of coastal towers, possibly because of the necessity to defend the coast with muskets because of a shortage of cannon when France became an ally of the Americans during the war of Independence (1776). The advantage of coastal towers was not taken seriously until a naval engagement at Mortella Point in Corsica in 1794 where a tower defied the Royal Navy. British military experts were impressed with the tower and, when Britain was faced with the same problem of enemy landings, the coastal tower was reconsidered and the first Martello Towers were built along the south east and later the east coasts of England. During the Napoleonic Wars both Guernsey and Jersey built towers with characteristics of their English counterparts.

This comparative study evaluates the building and structure of the towers, as well as their historical context, and traces the development of the early 'Pre-Martello' Guernsey towers into larger fortifications.

# Acknowledgements

| | |
|---|---|
| JOHN PENFOLD | Tutor and Inspiration for the original thesis. |
| PETER DAWSON | Help and encouragement |
| DR. GUY - *Army Museum* | For direction and advice. |
| GEORGE BRAMELL | For help with details on Fort George. |
| RONA COLE - *Guernsey Museum Curator* | For writing the Abstract. |
| LAURIE ADKINS | Guernsey Education Service. |
| BOB BURNS | Guernsey Museum Assistant Curator. |
| MARTIN TORODE - *Ex-Pupil* | Who started my interest in Martello Towers. |
| BERNARD HASSALL - *Priaulx Library* | For his help and photographs. |
| DR. TOMLINSON - *Priaulx Library* | For translating the De Garis Journal. |
| JOHN ROUSSEL | For translating Actes des Etats. |
| GEORGE LE FEUVRE | For translating Actes des Etats. |
| BRIAN GREEN - *Guernsey Press* | For photographs of Fortifications. |
| PAUL LE PELLEY | For help with south coast of England Towers and checking the script. |
| KEN TOUGH - *Greffier* | For help and advice. |
| STEPHEN FRANCIS - *Greffe Office* | For assistance with finding records. |
| COLIN PARTRIDGE - *Alderney* | For help with Alderney and WO records. |
| MARTYN BROWN - *Jersey Heritage Trust* | For help with Jersey Towers and photographs. |
| BILL DAVIES - *Jersey* | For help with the Jersey Towers. |
| PATRICIA BERRY - *Seaford Tower* | For help and information. |
| E. D. NORISS - *Royal Engineer Library* | For finding documents. |
| MARTIN WALSH | Photographs. |
| JOHN LLOYD - *Guernsey Teachers Centre* | For help with photocopying and information on the Brehon Tower. |
| CECIL ROUSSEL | For reading and checking for errors. |
| JOYCE BULLOCK | For typing dissertation. |
| TONY SEBIRE | For advising on printing and design. |

CROWN - COPYRIGHT material in the Public Records Office is reproduced by permission of the Controller of Her Majesty's Stationery Office.

# Contents

|  |  | *Page* |
|---|---|---|
| *ABSTRACT* | | 3 |
| *ACKNOWLEDGEMENTS* | | 4 |
| *CONTENTS* | | 5 |
| *INTRODUCTION* | | 7 |
| *Chapter 1:* | Martello Towers (Origin and English) | 13 |
| *Chapter 2:* | Pre-Martello Towers in Jersey and Guernsey 1778 | 17 |
| *Chapter 3:* | Later Towers in Guernsey 1804 | 29 |
| *Chapter 4:* | Jersey Martello Towers | 43 |
| *Chapter 5:* | Comparative Study - | |
| | *Jersey - Guernsey 1778* | 47 |
| | *Guernsey - England - Jersey 1804-1837* | 49 |
| | *Martello Towers Proposed but Not Built in C.I.* | 53 |
| *Chapter 6:* | Development of Guernsey Forts - | |
| | *Hougue à la Perre* | 55 |
| | *Mont Crevelt* | 57 |
| | *Houmet* | 63 |
| | *Saumarez* | 67 |
| | *Grey* | 67 |
| *Chapter 7:* | Building Materials | 71 |
| *Chapter 8:* | Guernsey Militia | 73 |
| | Armament of Forts and Towers | 73 |
| Chronological table of Events in the Channel Islands | | 88 |
| Pre-Martello Coastal Towers | | 90 |
| Guernsey Towers | | 91 |
| Bibliography | | 92 |
| Glossary of Military Terms | | 93 |
| INDEX | | 94 |

# The
# Channel
# Islands

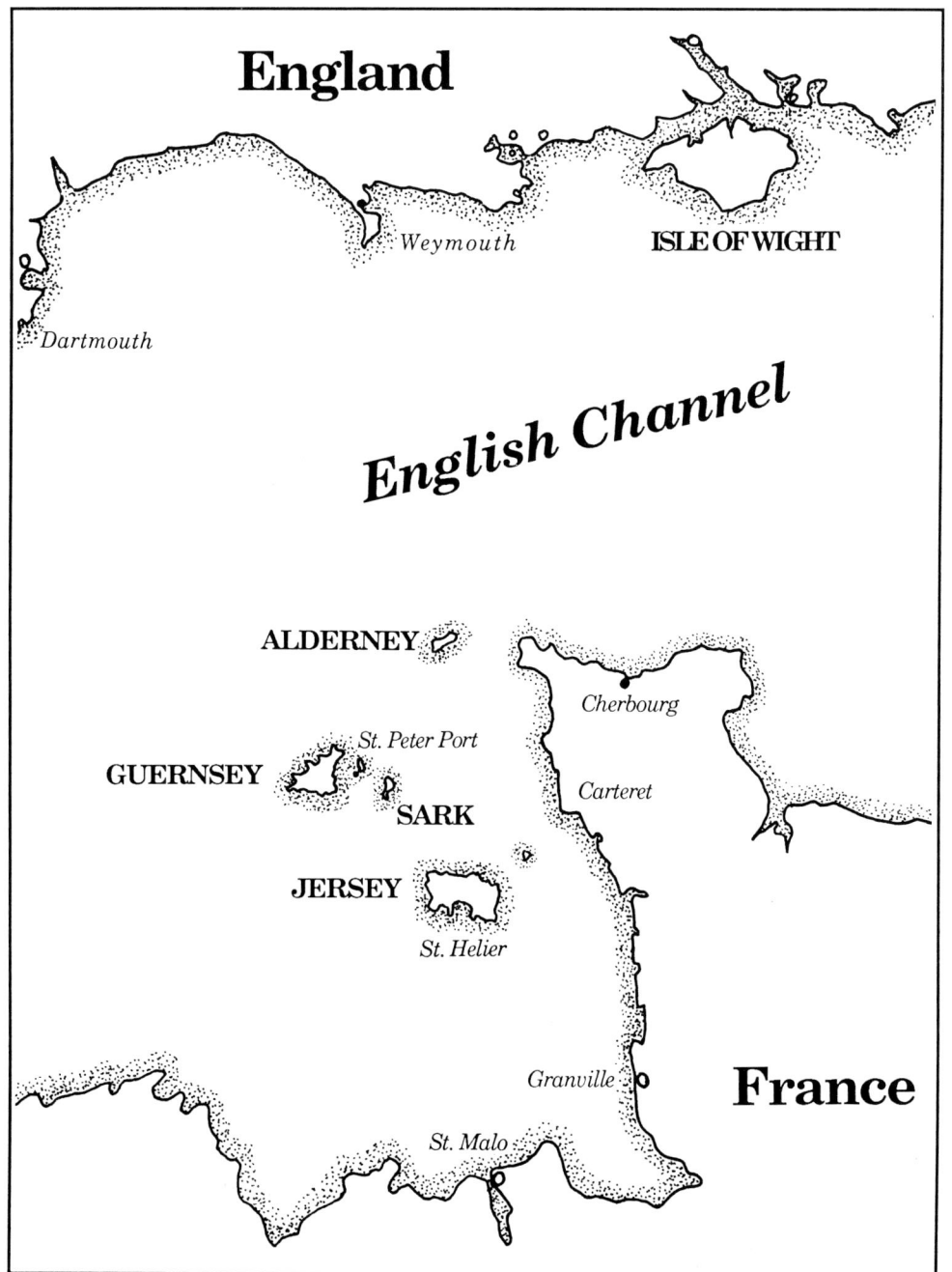

England

*Weymouth*       **ISLE OF WIGHT**

*Dartmouth*

**English Channel**

**ALDERNEY**

*Cherbourg*

*St. Peter Port*

**GUERNSEY**           *Carteret*

**SARK**

**JERSEY**

*St. Helier*

*Granville*       **France**

*St. Malo*

Map of the Channel Islands showing their close proximity to France and England.

# Introduction

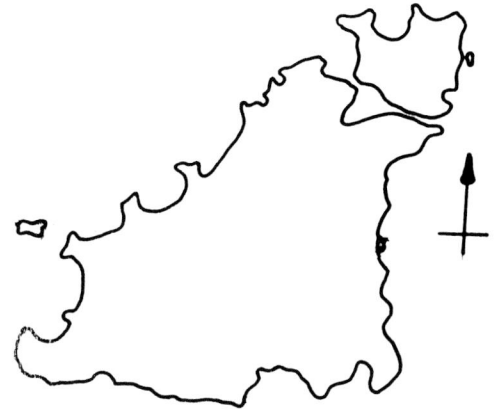

Guernsey, the second largest of the Channel Islands[1], situated as it is, so close to the French coast, owes as much to its Norman heritage as it does to the Crown of England. The Isles of Normandy, as the Channel Islands are called, formed part of the Duchy of Normandy and became linked with England in 1066 when William Duke of Normandy defeated Harold at the Battle of Hastings. The feudal system was already in existence in Guernsey, the Island was then divided, and given to two Vicomtes[2], who in turn allocated land to knights, later to be called Seigneurs[3]. Although the king of England surrendered the title of Duke of Normandy in 1259, the sovereign continued to rule the islands as though he was their Duke, observing their laws, customs and liberties. Successive Royal Charters have confirmed these privileges many of which can be traced back to feudal times including self government. This Norman heritage can be seen today in road and house names, as well as the spoken word -- Guernsey-French 'patois' can still be heard in the rural parts of the Island[4].

Over the centuries the French did their utmost to acquire the Islands, and in 1338 succeeded in capturing Castle Cornet and occupying it for five years. Again in 1356-7 the Island was in the hands of the French for a few months before they were driven out. Try as the French might, their occupation of the island was short lived. Forts around the island must date from this time, probably originally being made from earth sods and subsequently being built over and enlarged by successive improvements.

When the monarchy was returned to the throne, following the English Civil War, Charles II commissioned a military survey of the Channel Islands between 1678-1680 which was carried out by Colonel George Legge[5] and this is referred to in this script. In May 1685 the Lieutenant Governor complained to the Guernsey States that persons unknown had stolen iron, wood and doors from Vale Castle, and that the carriages and cannons on the Island had been vandalised. The States replied by issuing the following notice: "It is most strictly forbidden for anyone to touch, henceforth, the said cannons and carriages or to cause any damage or destruction or to pull down and demolish the fortifications and forts of this island subject to being severely chastised and corporally punished by Court orders; and it is also forbidden for any person, blacksmiths or others, to purchase wood or scrap iron from the said cannon carriages under a fine of one hundred crowns shared equally between the Crown and the informer; and all persons who know of any who have taken these things are requested to notify the Court so that such persons may be punished accordingly."[6] From this we can presume that the times were relatively peaceful, but that the old enemy was respected and the chief concern of Charles Macarty, Governor, was for a state of readiness in the Island.

1. Jersey is the largest and it is called with its smaller Island dependencies the Bailiwick of Jersey. Bailiwick of Guernsey consists of Alderney, Sark, Herm, Brechou, Jethou, Lihou.

2. Vicomtes - Norman word for Lord.

3. Seigneur's area of land is called a fief; this title is still held today.

4. Patois is a spoken, rather than a written language.

5. The first copy was lost overboard but later found, and now preserved at the Maritime Museum, Greenwich. A second copy is held at the British Museum. This copy is probably late 19th Century and held in the Bailiff's Library, Guernsey. There are differences between these copies and a certain amount of artistic licence, however, plans have found to be quite accurate.

6. Ordonnaces de la Cour Royale - May 1685, Page 221.

# Guernsey Militia

*Left Opposite.*
Officer, Grenadier Company,
1822.
*Right Opposite.*
Field Officer, Royal
Guernsey Artillery, 1895.

*Left Opposite:*
Gunner, Royal Guernsey
Artillery, 1787.
*Right Opposite:*
Sergeant , 3rd Regiment,
1867

Uniforms of the Royal
Guernsey Militia.

*With Permission of the Guernsey Post
Office Board, who printed stamps
from originals taken from 'The Royal
Guernsey Militia', J.P. Groves, 1895.
Priaulx Library, Guernsey.*

8

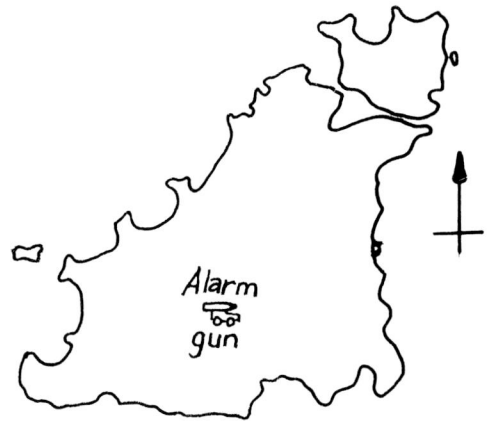

The Alarm Gun was positioned centrally in the Island.

The protection of the Channel Islands was first mentioned in 1203 during a war between King John and King Philip August II of France. The English King instructed Peter de Preaux to direct the feudal Lords to raise from their tenants a reasonable contingent for the defence of the Island; and a few weeks later, to take from the chief tenants a fifth of their incomes as a contribution "For the maintenance of soldiers to carry out the defence of the Islands."[7] An English garrison has been stationed almost continuously from this date onwards until 1940 in various forts established in the island. Victor Coysh in his book "Royal Guernsey" states, "It is impossible to date the formation of the Guernsey Militia," but goes on to suggest that it resulted from a system of manning watch stations. He believes that the militia was in an organised state in about 1340, rather than being just a band of semi-trained islanders. The Legge survey of 1680 took a poor view of the militia stating that it was not more than 1600 strong "being not well disciplined and worse armed." Their ammunition was useless, since the local arms were so varied, comprising of muskets, fuzees, carbines and blunder busses.[8] From 1750 onwards the militia was obviously important to the defence of the islands. With the threat of possible invasion, it was almost impossible to keep a large enough garrison to protect all the likely landing beaches, and difficult to quickly reinforce the garrison with men and supplies from England. This gave the militia an important role to play in the safety of the Island. Such was the fear of invasion that certain measures had been drawn up in the event of an enemy fleet approaching. An Alarm gun was to be sounded and the men were to report to their militia meeting places. Women undertook to wear red shawls and walk along the coast in order to deceive the enemy into over-estimating the strength of the land forces.[9]

These invasion fears were justified when, on the 1st May, 1779, the French attempted a landing at St. Ouen's Bay, Jersey. The invaders were vigorously repulsed "by the 78th regiment, seconded by the militia of the island, (so) that, after a faint, spiritless, and ill-supported resistance, they relinquished the enterprise."[10] Another attack took place in Jersey just under two years later, and very nearly succeeded. On the 5th January, 1781 the French landed at La Rocque and marched to St. Helier to arrive before the alarm had been raised.

The attempted invasion created excitement in the sister island of Guernsey, "......A cutter arrived from Jersey with startling intelligence, that a large body of French troops had landed in that island during the previous night, and were then in possession of St. Helier. The Lieutenant Governor Lieutenant Colonel Paulus Aemilius Irving instantly adopted the necessary measures for the defence of Guernsey, the militia were under arms all night, and the island under martial law."[11]

The following day another vessel arrived and reported that the invading force had been defeated. Papers found on a French general

7. *Priaulx Library: Festung Guernsey, Vol. IV.*

8. *Royal Guernsey 'A history of the Royal Guernsey Militia': Victor Coysh.*

9. *Guernsey Present and Past by Ralph Durand.*

10. *Bentleys Miscellany: Jersey Militia.*

11. *Guernsey Monthly Illustrated Magazine 1887 March.*

# Privateering

Prizes Brought into
Guernsey 1778

*By Permission of
Priaulx Library, Guernsey.*

revealed the fact that a corps of 14,000 men were ready on the coast of France, destined to land in Jersey in the first place, and then to invade Guernsey. It appeared to be the intention of the French government, once in possession of the islands, to have deported the inhabitants to Languedoc, and to have them replaced by a French population.

The attack on Jersey led to an increase in the fortifications around all of the islands' coasts. Some of the forts were paid for by the British treasury while small batteries were paid for by the States. The money was raised by taxing the inhabitants, and this duty was normally administered by the parish constables.[12] In addition to this the Parishes were often required to employ suitable masons and builders for the works. The Bulwarks were generally sited by the militia in consultation with the Governor or his adviser. However, this does not always seem to have been the case. In times of war the military advised and reported on the state of forts and batteries. This normally resulted in urgent work being paid for by the treasury but on some occasions the expense was shared. In 1780 a group of merchants and businessmen subscribed to the building of a fort near Paris Street which was known as "Fort Subscription" - later to be called Fort Amherst. A sum of £40 left over was to be spent on platforms at the fort.[13] (This is the only record of voluntary payment I have found). Because of the haphazard way in which the fortifications of the island were financed, ownership was questionable. The ownership of forts and land was finally resolved in 1847 when the Bailiff commissioned a report. This researched the land deeds and ownership, and, when complete, it was sent to the Lieutenant Governor. In 1848 forts were purchased by the States, with the notable exceptions of Castle Cornet and Fort George, which were purchased only after W.W.II.

The Channel Islands had been a constant annoyance to the French Navy, harbouring, as they did both privateers and the British Navy. Privateering is considered by most people as simply another word for piracy; but it was under the authorisation of the monarch with a letter of marque, and was subject to definite rules and regulations. After an enemy ship was captured her cargo was sold and the money realized was divided into stipulated shares: one-fifth went to the monarch, two-thirds of the remainder went to the owner of the vessel and one-third to the captain, officers and crew. Privateering was only enforced during times of war against enemy shipping and this practice continued until it was abolished in 1856 by Act of Parliament.

12. Constables meaning elected voluntary officers of the parish douzaine.

13. Actes des Etats 1780 Vol.11, Page 376.

INSTRUCTIONS for the Commanders of such Merchant Ships or Vessels who shall have Letters of Marque and Reprizals for private Men of War against the French King, his Vassals and Subjects, or others inhabiting within any of his Countries, Territories, or Dominions, by Virtue of Our Commission granted under Our Great Seal of Great-Britain, bearing Date the Fifth Day of August, 1778. Given at Our Court at St. James's, the Fifth Day of August, 1778, in the Eighteenth Year of Our Reign.

GEORGE R.

L.S.

ARTICLE I. THAT it shall be lawful for the Commanders of Ships authorized by Letters of Marque and Reprizal for private Men of War, to set upon by Force of Arms, and subdue and take the Men of War, Ships and Vessels, Goods, Wares and Merchandizes of the French King, his Vassals and Subjects, and others inhabiting within any of his Countries, Territories, and Dominions: But so as that no Hostility be committed, nor Prize attacked, seized, or taken, within the Harbours of Princes and States in Amity with Us, or in their Rivers or Roads, within the Shot of their Cannon, unless by Permission of such Princes or States, or of their Commanders or Governors in Chief in such Places.

ART.

Rules for Captain's of Merchant Vessels who have "Letters of Marque" for Privateering.

# Mortella
# Tower,
# Corsica

A sketch taken from an
original water colour,
painted by a member of the
services, soon after the
action by the British fleet
in 1794.

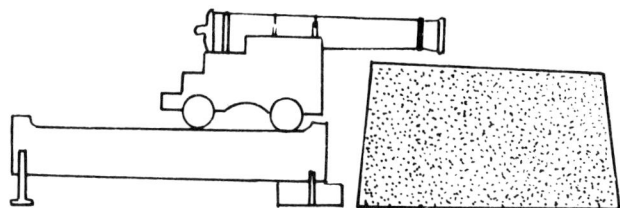

The 18 pounder is attached
to a carriage and mounted
upon a slide which pivots
on iron trucks to allow the
gun to be repositioned
quickly *(Early form of
Traversing platform)*.

# Chapter 1
# Martello Towers

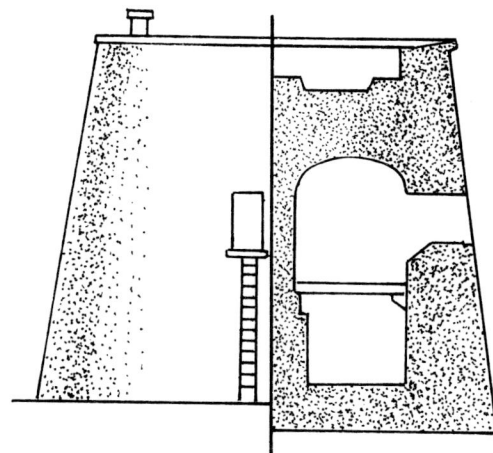

Elevation and section of Tower No. 13 in Hythe, Kent.

Over the centuries many different types of coastal fortifications have been built. Among the most interesting is the development of the Martello tower. This characteristic up-turned flower-pot-shaped redoubt resembles no other coastal fortification seen in Britain before. The purpose of the Martello Tower was to support coastal batteries and to resist invasions by land forces as well as, if necessary, to withstand a siege until reinforcements could be sought. Sheila Sutcliffe states in her book "Martello Towers" that "The towers were strategically placed to protect . . . vital installations and any particularly vulnerable stretch of coast where an invasion might be expected."[1] They were built to rigid designs by the army engineers and housed a small garrison[2] to give artillery support to, or to act in place of, the Navy. The long war with France which lasted almost continuously from 1793-1815 prompted the building of Martello towers first along the south east coast and later along the east coast of England.

The name Martello is a corruption of the word Mortella and was brought about by a naval engagement off the Islands of Corsica.[3] A round watch tower on Mortella Point in the Gulf of San Fiorenzo in 1794 held off the British Navy for two days of heavy fighting. Both the Navy and Military officers were deeply impressed by its resistance-especially as the garrison consisted of thirty-eight men and the armament was only one six-pounder and two eighteen pounder guns.[4]

Towers, as a means of coastal defence, became out-dated in Europe with the development of artillery power. It was only when Britain was faced with a new type of warfare, namely enemy landings from small craft in waters where battleships dare not venture,[5] that the idea of towers was reconsidered especially after the Mediterranean affair. The army was familiar with ordnance towers built in the late eighteenth century, although they were not common. Instances of small, circular, detached coastal towers being built before the classic Martello age began are of interest in showing not only that the idea was accepted, but also to show the development of the eventual design of the Martello Tower.

The Channel Islands were the first to build such fortifications in the late eighteenth century. From a military point of view the islands - Jersey, Guernsey, Alderney and Sark - are uncomfortably close to France and although they already had some coastal fortifications, many towers were built in 1778 to bolster these defences. The idea to build these round towers came from General Conway, Governor of Jersey. It is my belief that he instigated the towers because of the shortage of

1. *Martello Towers* by Sheila Sutcliffe, Chapter 1.
2. The garrison consisted of 30 men and officers.

3. These Mediterranean watch towers were built during successive centuries to warn the inhabitants of raids by pirates *Martello Towers*. Page 19.

4. The tower only surrendered due to a fire in the parapet. *Martello Towers*, Page 20.

5. Napoleon's plan to invade England was to build a fleet of flat bottom boats and to send a vast army to the English coast.

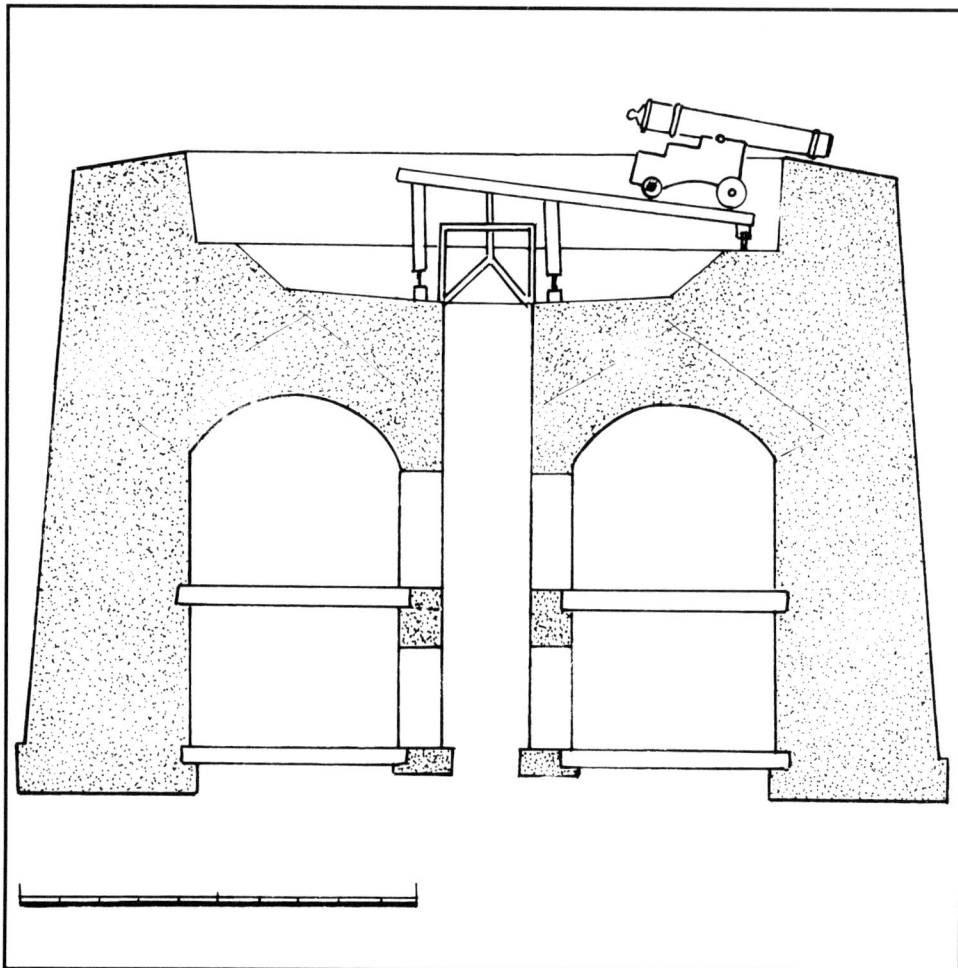

Martello Tower (section)
1804 as proposed at the
Rochester Conference on
coastal defence.
This is probably the
original drawing of the
tower untitled and to be
found in the Public Records
Office. (WO 55/778)

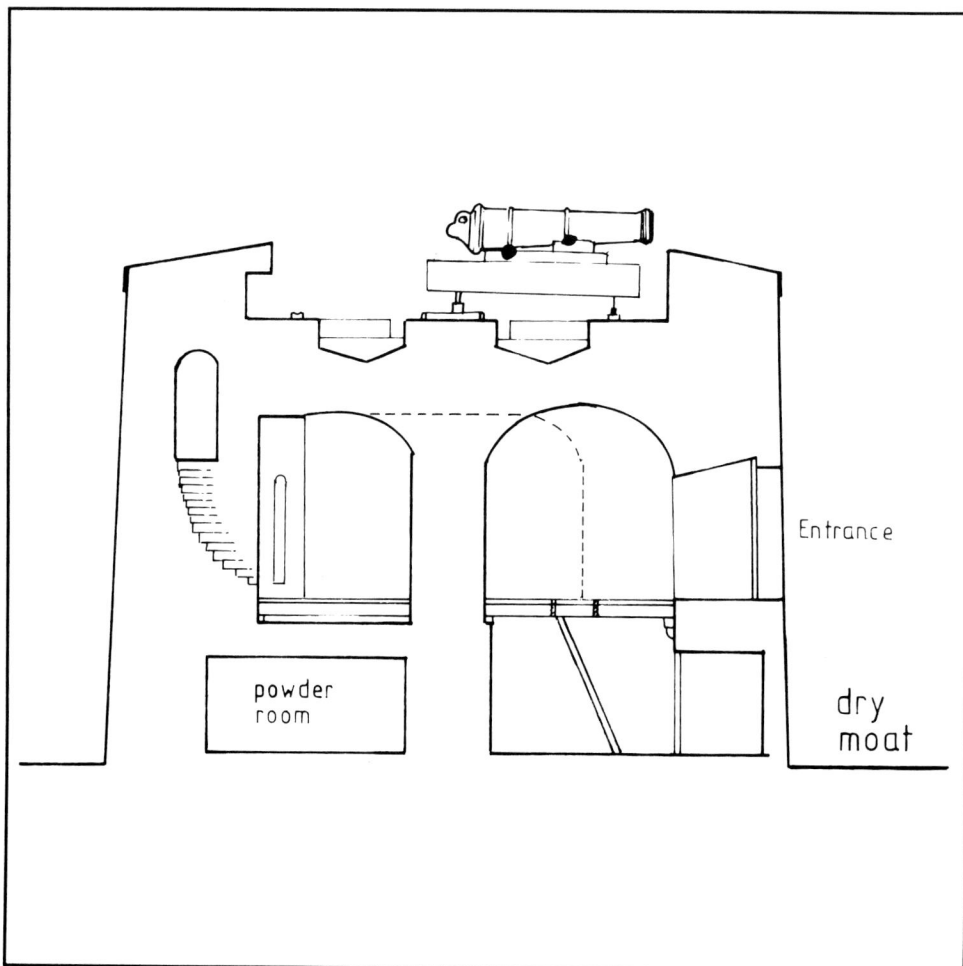

Entrance

powder
room

dry
moat

Martello Tower 73,
Wish Tower, Eastbourne.
*(Open to the Public)*

Martello Towers, Pevensey Bay.
(Reproduced from Illustrated London News, August 1889)

6. More details can be found in Chapters 2 and 6.

ordnance guns, and chose to design towers that could also be used by his soldiers to fire muskets from.[6] It is surprising that the towers built in Guernsey differ so much from the Jersey Towers, although they were built about the same time. It was proposed to build 30 towers in Jersey, (although only 23 were built - and one of these was square!), and 15 towers were proposed (and built) in Guernsey. Possibly the square tower proved to be too expensive to build because the local granite had to be trimmed square.

The fear of Napoleon's flotilla amassed at Boulogne prompted a review and survey of coastal defence plans. Britain's naval strategy was to blockade the French ports which made a surprise assault almost impossible. However, there was a danger that if the fleet was involved in another engagement, Napoleon might spring his attack. Various defensive plans were considered by the British: evacuating the inhabitants of coastal areas and using 'scorched ground policy,'[7] flooding the marshes by opening the sluice gates, building coastal sea towers (later to be called Martello towers), and constructing a military canal.[8]

7. Scorched ground - burning or destroying everything behind them.

8. This was not for transporting the army but delaying the advance by means of a wet ditch. 30 miles long from Shorncliff in Kent to the river Rotheral Rye Sussex, 1804.

When the war resumed in 1803 the public demanded better protection. A Captain Ford suggested a chain of towers as sea fortresses which he estimated would cost £3,000 each but this proposal met with numerous delays. He recommended that the towers should be sited to support existing batteries and to defend sluice gates. Eventually the plan was supported in principle by the Committee of Royal Engineers, but the final decision to build the towers was not made until 1805. The towers were eventually built along the south east coast of England between 1805-1812. Altogether some seventy-four towers were built along this coast. It was known that Napoleon's goal was to take London soon after an invasion of the south or south-eastern coast. Although it was doubtful if his flotilla stationed at Boulogne would have been able to negotiate the sea journey from France to the east coast of England, the inhabitants wanted protection along their coast line and there was always the threat of Napoleon diverting his soldiers to another port, and using bigger ships. In 1808 more towers were built along the east coast. These were larger and carried more armament than the south coast towers. In total twenty-nine towers were built. These were lettered (A,B,C, etc.) whereas the south coast towers were numbered (1, 2, 3, etc.).

In Guernsey, General Doyle, Lieutenant Governor, innovated a design for three towers to be built on the west coast of Guernsey. This was in 1804 and so these pre-date the towers built in England. These towers were larger than the towers built in 1778 and were without loop-holes. They were built specifically to carry a gun on the top of the tower and to house a small garrison. Although they were reported to have been poorly built, it is surprising that no report was commissioned to evaluate their merits and/or de-merits prior to the commencement of the English south coast towers.

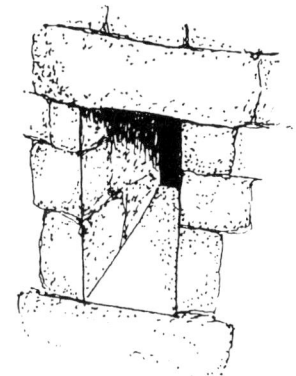

Loop holes for firing muskets from in 1778 Towers

# Towers of the South and East Coast of England

Map showing tower positions on the South-East Coast of England. Some towers are open to the public.

## SOUTH EAST COAST TOWERS STILL STANDING

1. East Wear Bay on cliff nr. Folkestone.
2. On knoll inland 50 ft below tower 1.
3. On cliff above Copt Point.
4. In private house extreme western end of the Leas.
5. In grounds of School behind Sandgate High Street.
6.
7. } Towers in Shorncliffe Camp area.
8.
9.
13. Western end of West Parade, Hythe.
14.
15. } These towers stand in the middle of flat land where the Hythe firing
19. ranges are sighted.
23. Romney marsh.
24. } West end of Dymchurch,
25. these guard Marshland sluice gates.
28. Rye Harbour.
30. West of Rye, Winchester Road.
55. Norman's Bay.
60. Pevensey Bay.
61.
62. } Pevensey Bay area.
64.
66. Just east of Langney Point.
73. Wish Tower in Devonshire Park.
74. Seaford. Added in 1808.

## EAST COAST TOWERS STILL STANDING

A. St. Osyth Stone.
C. Bush Wall Point.
D. Outskirts of Clacton nr. Jaywick.
E. Clacton built on Clacton Wash.
F. Clacton Cliffs on the Marine Parade.
K. Overlooking Walton Backwaters.
L. On peninsular between Stour and Orwell.
M. Overlooks river Orwell.
N. Opposite bank to M. Part of three tower formation.
P. West end of Felixtowe.
Q. Southwest extremity of Bulls Cliff.
T. } These towers on the mouth of the
U. river Deben overlooking Woodbridge Haven.
W. Nr. Bawdsey Parish on low cliffs.
Y.
Z. } Between Bawdsey Beach to
AA. Shingle Street.
CC. One mile south of Aldeburgh at Slaghden.

16

## Chapter 2
# Pre-Martello Towers in Jersey and Guernsey 1778

The early towers built in the Channel Islands are often referred to as "Martello Towers," a corruption of the word Mortella explained in the last chapter. Perhaps they are better described as round coastal towers, although in practice they were largely used as guard/barrack, watch towers. Their purpose was to support coastal batteries at possible landing places.

In 1778 when the French became the allies of the Americans in their War for Independence, General Seymore Conway, Governor of Jersey, was certain that the French would seize the opportunity and attack the Channel Islands. So, in May he wrote to Lord Weymouth, Secretary of State, proposing the construction of 30 coastal towers to protect the coast of Jersey. He described the towers as needing to be 30' - 40' high and spaced 500 yards apart with the walls pierced with loop holes for musketry in two stages. They were designed to resist enemy landings and to be out of range (at that time) of ships' guns. The letter continues "The design was supported by Marshall Saxe, he has seen a square tower hold for 2-3 days . . . . . Towers gave trouble at the Havannah on Lord Albermacles expedition and could not be taken until a frigate was brought in to batter it . . . . .These towers here would annoy the enemy excessively in their boats and in our principle bays could not be battered by their ships as the shores there are very flat." The letter continued to point out that "the batteries and entrenchments would make it very difficult for the enemy to establish himself. . . . . . They would give a great degree of protection and confidence to our troops disposed in the entrenchments and batteries."[1]

It would seem that General Conway designed the towers himself, although to date no documentation has been found to substantiate this.[2] The towers proposed would protect the beaches and also give a height advantage, useful when being used as observation posts.

In June 1778 Lord Weymouth passed an extract of Conway's letter to Lord Amherst, Master-General of the Ordnance, asking for an estimate of the cost of such a building programme.[3] On the 3rd July the Board of Ordnance informed Lord Weymouth that the cost would be £156 per tower.[4] Just two days later Lord Weymouth signified "the King's pleasure for thirty towers" to be erected in Jersey at a cost of £4,680. There seems to have been a delay in building the Jersey towers as H. R. S. Pocock, in his paper[5], concludes that none of the Jersey towers were completed before 1779. However, in a letter, General Conway wrote -- " . . . of the 30 towers order'd 4 are as yet completed, indeed properly but two of those order'd by (the) Government, the other two being built chiefly at the expense of the Island and there are two more begun. The reason given by the Lieutenant Governor (Conway's Deputy) why they have not gone on

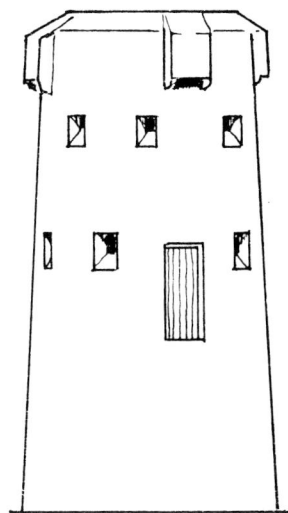

JERSEY TOWER

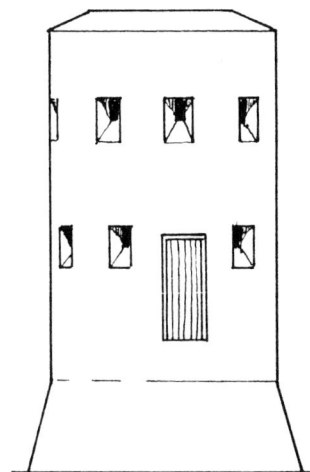

GUERNSEY TOWER

*1. P.R.O. W.O. 46/10 20th May, 1778.*

*2. General Conway could have given an outline specification to the Captain Bassett to arrange for plans to be made, but there is no evidence. Jersey Societe 1971.*

*3. P.R.O. W.O. 46/10 13th June, 1778 Lord Weymouth's letter to Lord Amherst, Master-General of the Ordnance.*

*4. P.R.O. W.O. 55/372 3rd July, Board of Ordnance to Lord Weymouth, 5th July, Lord Weymouth to Jersey.*

*5. Jersey Societe 1971 "Jersey Martello Towers" H. R. S. Pocock. Page 288.*

# St. Brelade, Jersey

View of St. Aubin's Town and Harbour taken near the 3rd Tower.

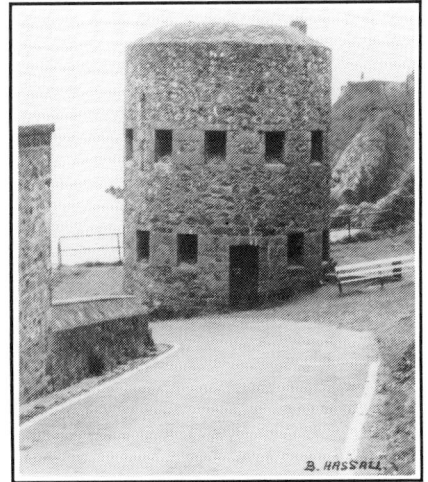
Tibo Tower at Petit Bôt Bay

faster, besides the want of materials and convoy, has been that the Masons there being a great number of them Farmers, could not be kept constantly to the work . . . . . .in the winter as they have done in Guernsey which has forwarded their work greatly . . . . . . The Magistrates of Jersey have given an order for the masons to work at no private work; but Captain Bassett[6] represents that the number in the island is not sufficient to finish them with any expedition in which case I should hope a number might be order'd from England to assist."[7]

On the 17th July, 1778 Lord Weymouth again signified the King's pleasure for fifteen towers to be erected in Guernsey " . . . . . . of the same form and mode as those ordered for the Island of Jersey."[8] Five days later the Board of Ordnance ordered Captain Bassett to proceed with erecting the towers,[9] such was the urgency of protecting the Islands so close to France.

Work started almost at once in Guernsey. Nicholas de Garis records in his journal[10] that work commenced on the 31st August, 1778. A large workforce was employed; eighteen masons were reported as working during the construction of one tower a total of 593 man days. Mathieu Tostevin seems to have been the forman, as he was the only mason employed throughout the building of the tower. The total number of days spent by the Carrieurs (stonedressers) amounted to 274 days and of this total 52 days were spent prior to the commencement proper. Serviteurs de Masons (labourers) were employed for a total of 372 days. From this record it is almost possible to visualise the involvement of the labour force in this project. At a meeting of the Société, 21st February, 1906, it was then estimated that the cost of building the tower at Petit Bôt was about £100 sterling (1,339 livres tournois).[11]

It seems impossible but (according to an old De Garis diary[12] it was the case) the 15 towers were completed within 7-8 months. As the entry records:-
*"The towers of Guernsey were started about the Feast of St. Michel (September) 1778 and finished in March 1779."*

Having researched this period in the Public Record Office in England I can find no entry to confirm the completion date of the towers. Ledgers of the time only refer to 'Works in Guernsey.' It can only reasonably be assumed that the Guernsey towers were completed before those in Jersey.

The story is picked up again in the Actes des Etats: On the 30th September, 1778 the States resolved:- "To acquire three pieces of land, at States expense, requested by the said Lieutenant Governor, on which to build three Towers which His Majesty the King in his kindness has ordered, with others, to be built at His Governments expense for the defence of this island.[13] 1° One tower on land . . . . . . at Mont Crevelt, 2° One tower . . . . . at La Hougue à la Perre, 3° One tower . . . . . . at La Hougue-a-la-pere, and for this purpose they nominate and authorise

6. Capt. Bassett was the resident Engineer in the Channel Islands - Stationed in Jersey and transferred in 1779 to Guernsey.

7. P.R.O. W.O. 34/105 Letter from General Conway to Lord Amherst, 19th January, 1779.

8. P.R.O. W.O. 55/372 Letter 17th July 1778 from Lord Weymouth.

9. P.R.O. W.O. 47/92 22nd July, 1778 Board of Ordnance.

10. Nicholas de Garis Journal - Priaulx Library, Guernsey. (See pages 20, 22 and 23 for translation of script).

11. Guernesiaise Societe (1906) Vol. 5 meeting 21st February: Original journal found and translated from French. Journal of Nicholas de Garis (Procureur of the Pauvres of the Forest Parish) 1777 - 1786. (Livres tournois was the Guernsey currency of the day).

12. De Garis Diary. Page 109 - Priaulx Library.

13. Actes des Etats, 30th September , 1778(translated from French) (Acts of the States)

19

# Time Sheet

Journal du bastiste de la tour de Petitbo[?] Commencée le 3[1]
Avoust 1778

Jours d'ouvriers marquez ci despous

**Masons**

| | 31 | 1 | 2 | 3 | 4 | 5 | 6 | 7 | 8 | 9 | 10 | 11 | 12 | 13 | 14 | 15 | 16 | 17 | 18 | 19 | 20 | 21 | 22 | 23 | 24 | 25 | 26 | 27 | 28 | 29 | 30 |

Pierre Tostevin
Mathieu Tostevin
Jean Tostevin
Alexandre Tostevin
Jaques Tostevin
Thomas Tostevin
Pierre Falaise
Mathieu Tostevin
Pierre Robert
Thomas Le huray
Jean Le Lacheur
Pierre Gallienne
Nicolas Brehaut
Thomas Le Page
Massy Robert
Nicolas Martin
Daniel Mollet
Auguste Thoume

Carrieurs
Jean Alicaume
Jean Guéripel
Charles Rose
Wm Rose
Jean Tostevin
Elie Guéripel
Pierre Mollet

Serviteurs de masons
Samuel de Larue
Leonard Leray
Jean Tostevin
Pierre Guéripel fs P.
Pierre Guéripel fs Jn
Pierre Robert
Jean Falaize
Pierre De Moullepié
Jean Rose
Nicolas Maugeur
Jean Brehaut
Elie De Larue

Detailed record of hours worked by the various craftsmen.

De Garis Journal, Priaulx Library, Guernsey.

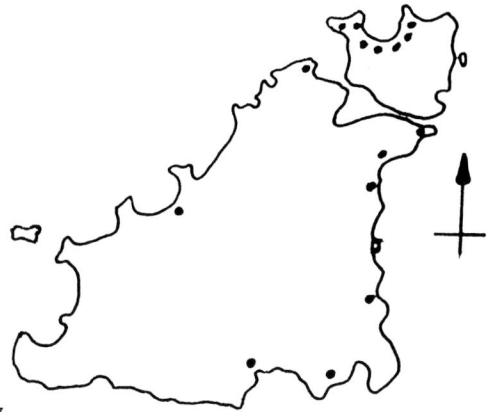

Map of Guernsey showing positions of pre-Martello Towers.

William Le Marchant, Esq., Charles Andros, Esq. and Pierre De Jersey to acquire the said sites and to negotiate with the said owners as to prices and to obtain the best possible conditions of sale. And since the building of the said Towers in the stated places is considered essential and necessary for the security and defence of this island, the States are of the opinion that, if the said owners of anyone of them refuses to sell their lands of any piece of land, the said towers should be built, notwithstanding a Clameur de Haro[14] or any opposition whatsoever and the said Landowners would receive compensation according to respective values. And, in that event, the said authorised persons would call in experts for the purpose of fixing valuations of the said sites." From this it can be seen that the land was compulsorily purchased and the Clameur de Haro overruled, such was the importance given to this project for the security of the island.

The reason for only three pieces of land being purchased, according to James Marr in his book, "Bailiwick Bastions", was because "many of the fortifications having been erected upon Commons which was public property, or upon the coast within the limits which belong to the Community above high water mark, no documents were required by the States to ensure their title to the land."[15]

No other information has been found to date regarding the building of the 15 towers. It would seem that fortifications were still being built when Captain Bassett wrote to the Board of Ordnance in 1780 expressing his concern that "the States have allowed that one-third only of the masons formerly employed by the Kings works might work upon (sic) and that these not being compelled would not work without any increase of wages; that the Peasants refuse to Quarry stones from their rocks and that he therefore proposed that Bricklayers . . . . . . maybe sent in the Spring to finish the works next summer."[16] The Board replied to his request by suggesting that workmen be employed from among the troops, in accordance with regulations, and that materials be sought elsewhere. In November, Captain Bassett again reported to the Ordnance saying he had found a field of clay and requested "40 good bricklayers and 15 brickmakers to be sent from England." A Mr. James Trimmer was sent to investigate the price at which bricks could be made and to report back to the board. He estimated that 6,000,000 bricks could be made for £36 per million. The Board, replying to the request for men, sent 20 bricklayers and suggested the local authorities employ the rest by the day.[17] At this time numerous fortifications were being built, including Fort George. This obviously strained the Island's building resources as it was a prosperous era with Privateering, Wine and Spirit trades increasing demand for private building and as these letters indicate the result was a delay in the building of the fortifications. The only confirmation that all 15 towers were built by 1787 was that all are shown on the surveyed map, commissioned by the Duke of Richmond.

14. Clameur de Haro is a Norman custom which remains law in the island to-day. If anyone wishes to refrain a neighbour from encroaching on his property, he obtains two witnesses and in their presence and on his knees crys "Haro, Haro, Haro, a l'aide mon prince! On me fait tort" and then the Lord's prayer is said in French. This appeal has to be respected and the action must cease, until the case can be heard in Court. The grievance must be put in writing and lodged at the Greffe within twenty four hours.

15. Bailiwick Bastions, L. James Marr Page 47 Source: Report on fortifications January 6th, 1847 by Thomas Retilley, Thomas F. de Havilland to the Bailiff Peter Strafford Carey.

16. P.R.O. W.O. 47/96 Surveyor General Minute Book 24th September 1780 Ref. 796.

17. P.R.O. W.O. 47/97 Minutes of the Board of Ordnance, 12th May 1781.

# The Journal

The detailed Journal of Nicholas de Garis, 1778, showing the carting days.

TRANSLATION FROM FRENCH OF THE JOURNAL OF NICHOLAS DE GARIS

CARTING DAYS

|  | * £. | s. |
|---|---|---|
| Sieur Daniel Naftel 1 day 11th Sept. (carting) stone | 7. | 00 |
| Item Elie Queripel the same day " | 7. | 00 |
| Ditto 14th the 2 carts to town for timber | 14. | 00 |
| Ditto 15th " " 1 day (carting) stone | 14. | 00 |
| Ditto 17th Sieur Daniel brought a cartload of timber from town | 7. | 00 |
| Ditto 18th 2 carts 1 day carting stone | 14. | 00 |
| Ditto 21st the 2 carts each brought a load of lime | 7. | 10 |
| Ditto 23rd Elie Queripel carting some stone | 7. | 00 |
| Ditto 25th the 2 carts 1 day (carting) stone | 14. | 16 |
| Ditto 30th the 2 carts 1 day (carting) stone | 9. | 16 |
| Item 3 days carting stone | 14. | 14 |
| Item 7 loads of bricks | 49. | 00 |
| Item 2 loads of lime | 7. | 10 |
| Item 4 loads of shingle | 28. | 00 |

|  | £. | s. |
|---|---|---|
| On Friday 25th Sept. were delivered 18 loads of blue stone at 8½ shillings a load and carting | 107. | 2 |
| Item Wednesday 30th the same 7 loads | 41. | 13 |
| Item Monday 5th Oct. 1 cartload | 5. | 19 |
|  | 154. | 14 |
|  | 5. | 19 |
| Ditto 6th 1 cartload | 160. | 13 |
| Oct. 22 arrived 2325 bricks at 40 shillings a thousand | 65. | 2 |

|  | £. | s. |
|---|---|---|
| Sept. 25th arrived at Tibo 22 dozen blue stones @ 4 shillings a dozen | 61. | 12 |
| Ditto 30th 6½ dozen | 16. | 16 |
| October 5th 1 dozen | 2. | 16 |
| Item 1 dozen @ 4 shillings | 81. | 4 |
|  | 2. | 16 |
|  | 84. | 00 |

N.B. Authors Note: This is livres tournois not sterling.

|  | £. | s. |
|---|---|---|
| Ditto 2nd arrived 400 bushels of lime @ 14 sous a bushel | 280. | 00 |
| Item for carting of 350 bushels of the said lime @ 3 sous a bushel | 52. | 10 |
| Item burnt to extract from stone 10 £ of powder | 7. | 00 |
| October 14 Received 50 bushels of lime | 35. | 00 |
| The lining of the top and the cost of lockers | 78. | 8 |
| September 12 received from Sieur Jean Melich six guineas | 88. | 4 |
| Ditto 19th Received from the said Melich 8 guineas | 117. | 12 |
| Ditto 26th Received 1 guinea | 14. | 14 |
| Oct. 3rd Received 5 guineas | 73. | 10 |
| Ditto 10th Received £40. 12s. 10d. sterling | 567. | 12 |
| Item received twice eleven guineas | 161. | 14 |
| Item 31 received nine guineas | 132. | 6 |
| Item No. 14 received £19. 6. 4½ sterling | 270. | 9.4 |
| Item received 4 guineas 4 penys | 59. | 0.0 |

|  | £. | s. | d |
|---|---|---|---|
| Sept. 12 paid stone dressers | 40. | 19. | 6 |
| Item paid builders labourers until the said day | 48. | 16. | 0 |
| Item 19th paid the said labourers until the said day | 48. | 00. | 0 |
| Item 25 nails | 00. | 12. | 0 |
| Ditto 26 paid the said labourers | 44. | 16. | 0 |
| Item paid the said labourer in 4 weeks | 133. | 12. | 0 |
| Item paid " " for 1 week | 30. | 8. | 0 |
| Item for 54 days that I Nicholas de Garis junior have been supervisor of works at 2 shillings a day | 75. | 00. | 0 |
| Item 5 days labourers | 4. | 00. | 0 |

Translation from French of the Journal of Nicholas de Garis

# Tower
# Plan

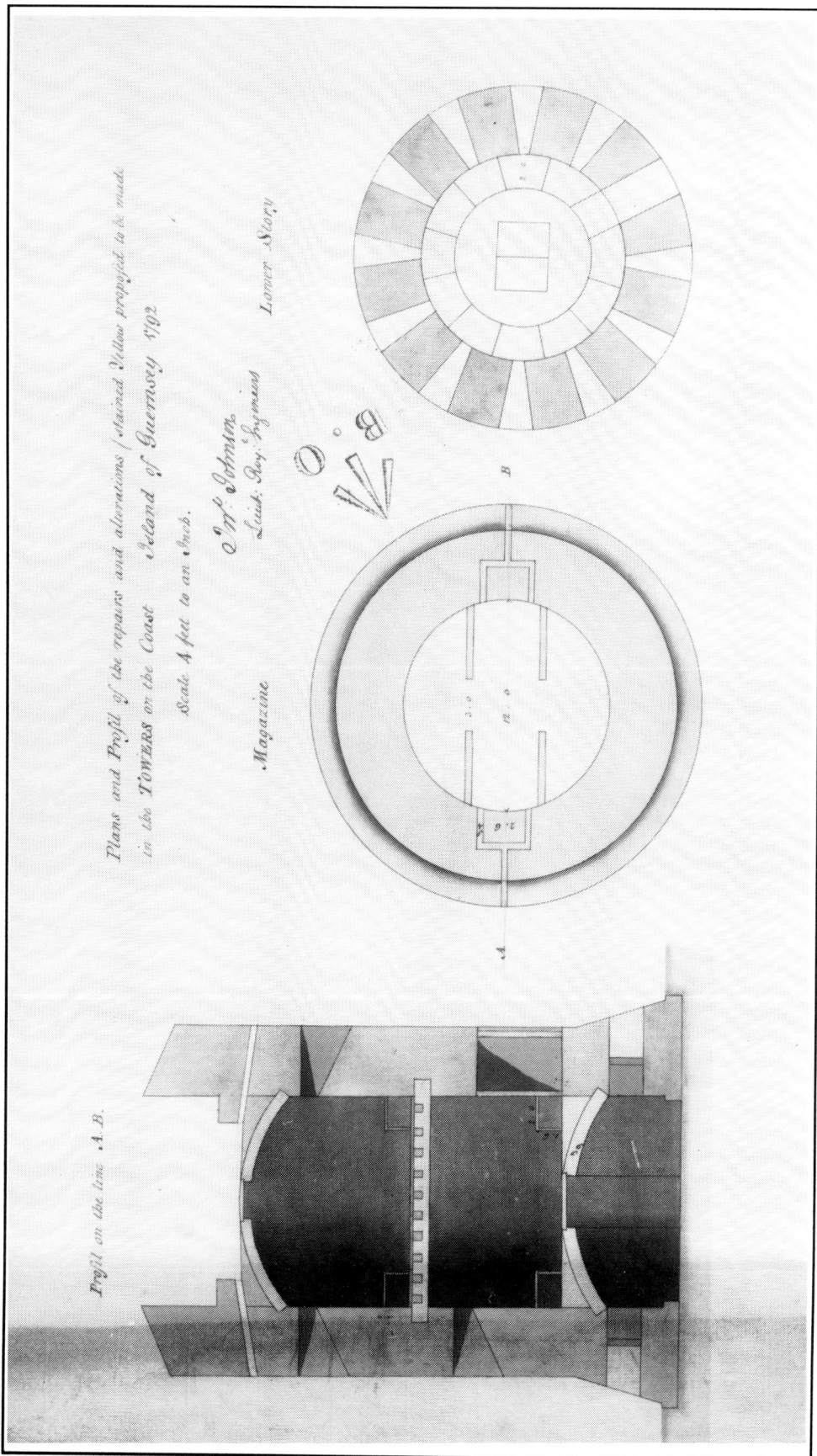

Plans and Profil of the repairs and alterations / stained Yellow propos'd to be made
in the TOWERS on the Coast    Island of Guernsey 1792.

Scale 4 feet to an Inch.

2.N.º Johnson.
Lieut. Roy. Engineers

Magazine          Lower Story

Profil on the line A.B.

Plans and profile of
proposed alterations and
repairs to Guernsey Towers
in 1792.

*Public Records Office
Ref. WO 78/1191 S BC/2737*

24

Tower No. 14 overlooking Saints Bay.

18. P.R.O. W.O. 55/808 Report 1787.

In 1787 a report was ordered "upon the best mode of Defence for the Island of Guernsey in general."[18] It was recommended that several landing places be fortified by establishing batteries on commanding points "So as to annoy an enemy on his approach, and bring a crossfire in front of the intrenchments. This in part done and many batteries already executed, the situations of some of which are well chosen, but we cannot think the towers we found near these batteries afford sufficient protection to them, since from their circular figure, and smallness of their diameter, the fire from the Creneaux, and even from the top is very inconsiderable (sic) . . . . . . we approve of Towers, but would recommend a different construction." The report was signed by Robert Morse, Abraham D'Aubant and I. Evelegh. Sheila Sutcliffe, points out that two of these officers, Lieutenant Colonel Robert Morse (who later became Inspector-General of Fortifications) and Lieutenant Colonel Abraham D'Aubant, (who saw action later in Corsica and would have known about the Mortella Point engagement), served on a committee of Royal Engineers called upon to advise on the sites and design for the south coast towers in England in 1803.

One puzzle remains on the building of these pre-martello towers. Why did Captain Bassett, after being ordered by the Board of Ordance to build the Guernsey towers in the "same mode and form as those ordered in Jersey", make them smaller? Was it simply because the Guernsey towers were built first? Records of this period are incomplete and it seems that missing information holds the answer. French attacks were certainly planned on the islands but we cannot be sure to what extent the towers acted as a deterrent.

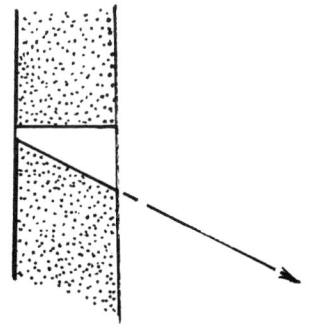

Angle of fire

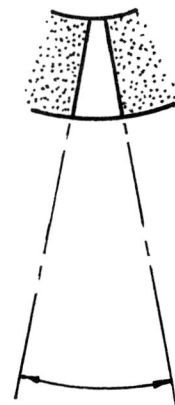

Field of fire

25

# Map of Guernsey 1802

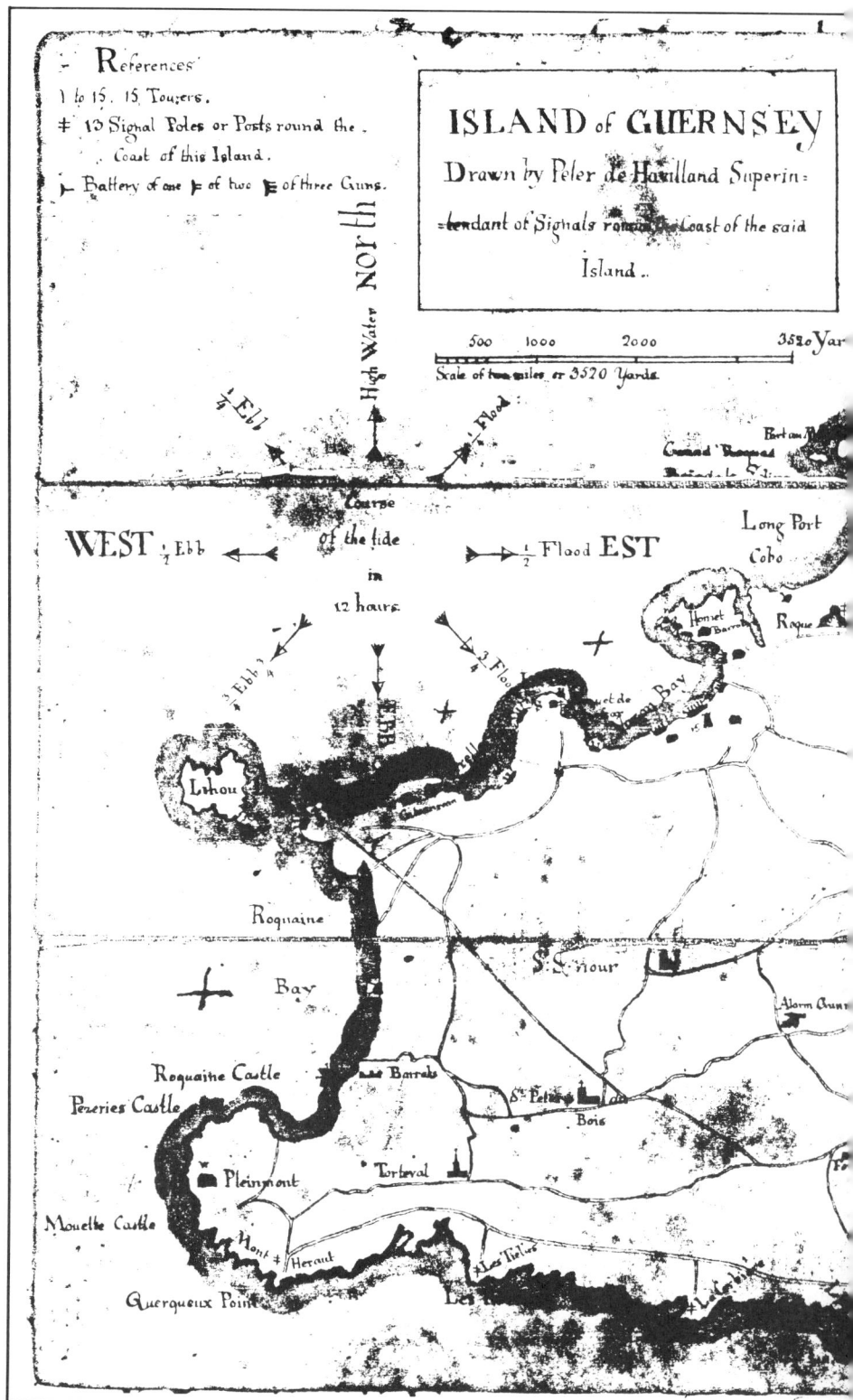

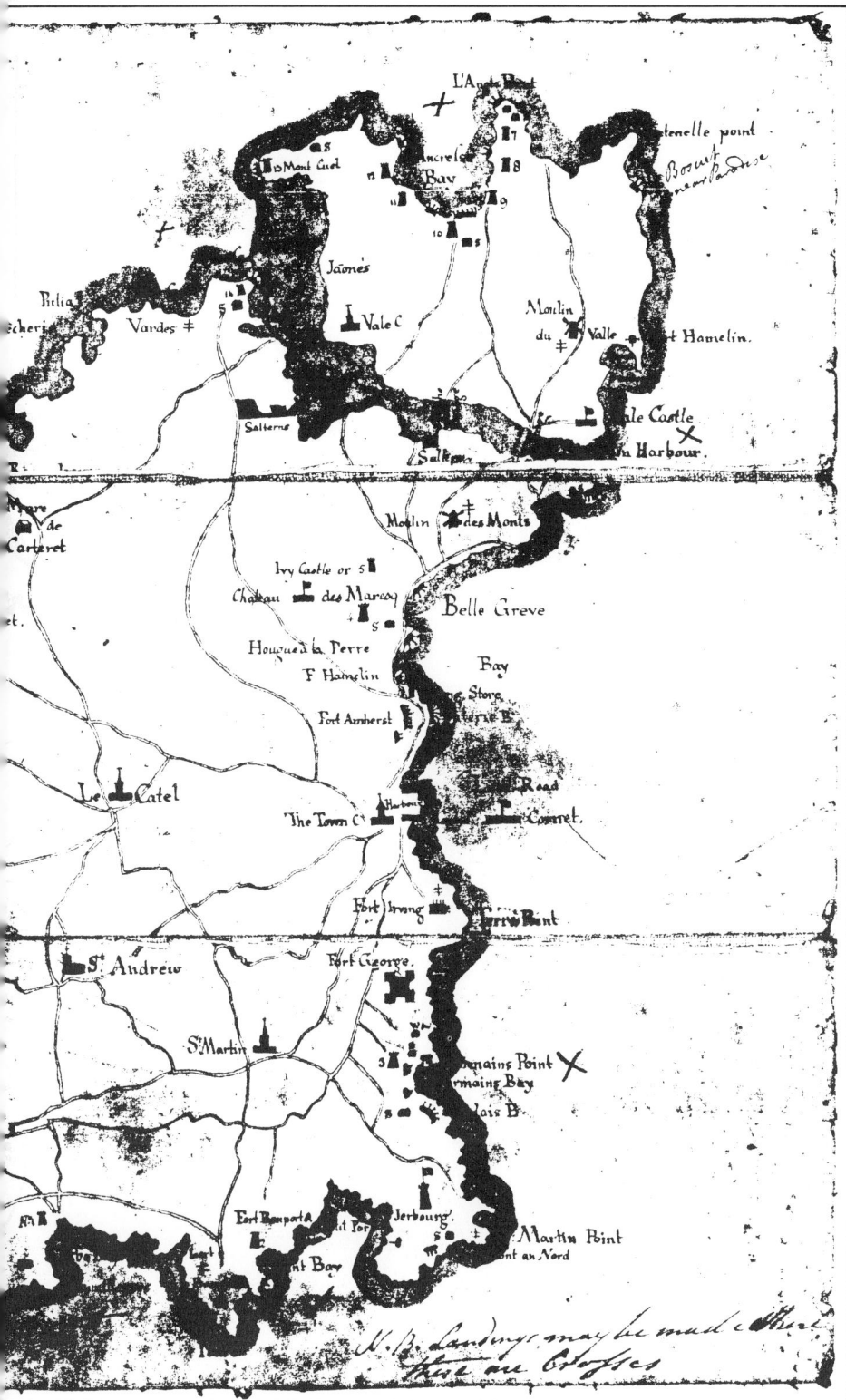

Map accompanying the 1802 Report referred to in this chapter, showing possible landing sites and anchorage places.

*Public Records Office*
*Ref. WO33/77*

# Fort
# Grey

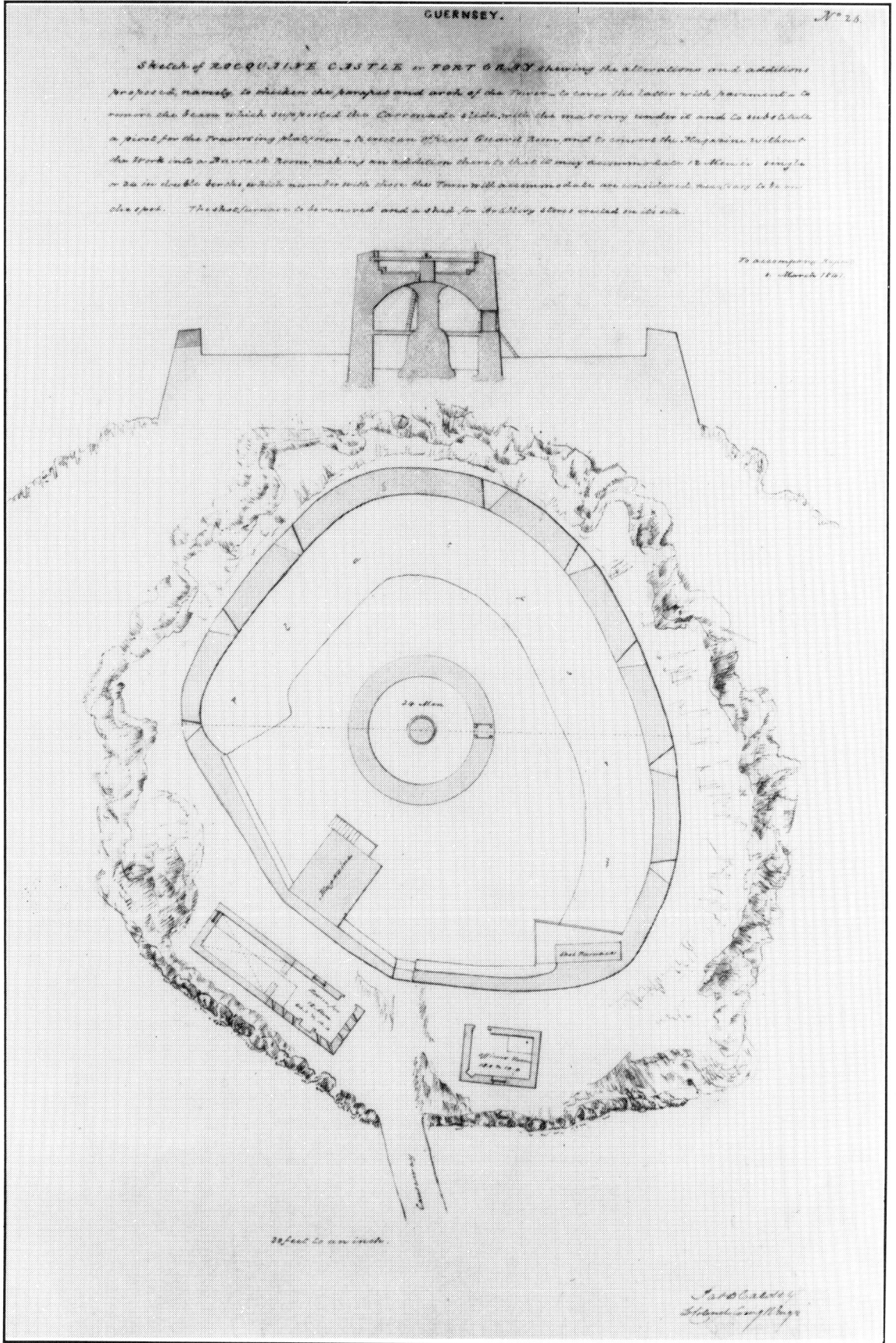

Plan of
Rocqaine Castle
or Fort Grey,
Guernsey

# Chapter 3
# Later Towers in Guernsey 1804

Fort Grey built in 1804.

The Peace of Amiens, signed in 1802, eased the situation only temporarily since war recommenced fourteen months later. During this unsettled period with the immediate threat of invasion withdrawn, reports on the state of defence in the islands were drawn up. Major John Humphrey R. E. suggested that "tides, winds and running tide . . . (could well determine). . . when and where an attack would be made."[1] In his report Humphrey referred to the importance of the Channel Islands to the trade routes and mentioned the stationing of scout boats as well as gun ships to secure a safe passage. "The Enemy could take advantage of tides therefore provision must be made to defend the beaches". He enclosed a tide timetable to his superiors and made reference to the one mile difference between the high and low tide marks. An attempt to gain control of the Islands, he believed, would be made whenever a war between England and France broke out. He went on to say that "To prevent landing being effected on the coast of this Island (Guernsey) numerous batteries have been erected." He also enclosed a plan and strongly recommended that these works or others adapted to this ground by better judgement than his "May be carried into execution during the time of Peace which is the only time they can be carried on to advantage . . . . . I also beg to recommend that an order may be given for the guns in all batteries in the Island to be examined and reported on as many are supposed not fit for service." He went on to press home the point "All the works that are considered necessary for the defence of the Island ought to be kept up equally in time of Peace as in war." It is obvious from this report that Guernsey and the other islands felt threatened because of their close geographic position to France, particularly Jersey, which Humphrey referred to as an advanced port which might be taken before it was put into a state of defence.

In 1803 the Government sent two proven military men to the Channel Islands to serve as representatives of the Governor:- Lt. Governor General Don in Jersey and Lt. Governor Major General Sir John Doyle, in Guernsey. Doyle's first task was to reinforce his island's defences. This improvement required the earth sod banks[2] to be replaced by stone and brick ones. Lieutenant Colonel Mackelcan, Commander Royal Engineers, compiled a comprehensive report on the state of the Islands.[3] The report detailed the coastal defences giving the condition of each battery and tower. It included suggested improvements to Rocquaine Castle and stated "There appears to be a space sufficient in the rear of the Battery for a small Barrack or Tower." With regard to L'Eree (a telegraph point) the report states "the idea is to make the present Battery unassailable by scarfing the rock on which it is situated, and erecting a Tower on its gorge for the accommodation of the Garrison intended to be stationed in it."

1. P.R.O. W.O. 30/57 25th November 1802 Defence of the Channel Islands.

2. P.R.O. W.O. 55/1549 Report 1803.

3. P.R.O. W.O. 30/57 Coastal defences 1803 Full Report.

# Plan of Guernsey

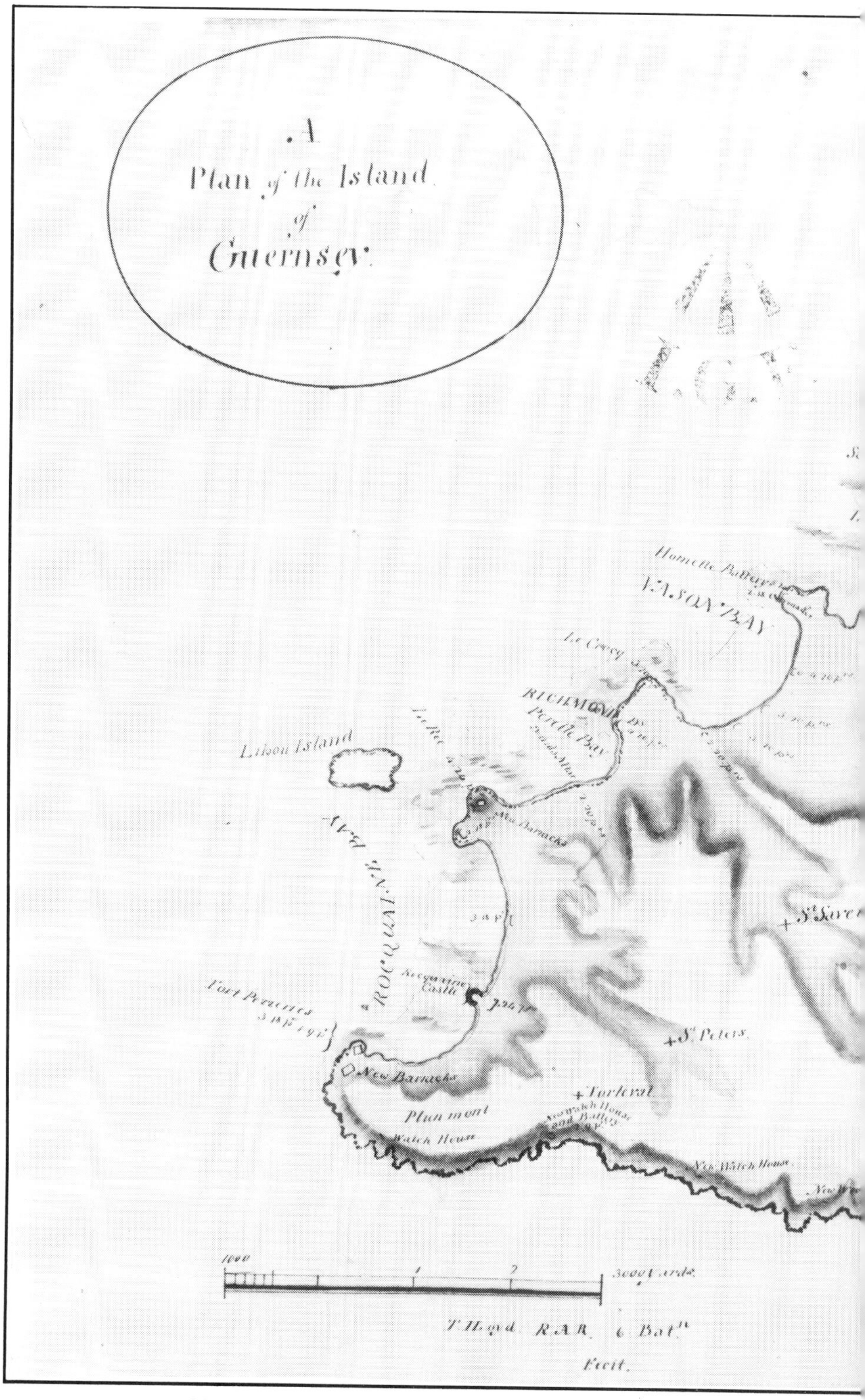

A Plan of the Island of Guernsey

VASON BAY

Hamette Battery

Le Crecy

RICHMOND
Pearle Bay

Lihou Island

Le Ree

Martello Barracks

ROCQUAINE BAY

+ S.t Sore

3 & F.t

Acquaine Castle

+ S.t Peters

Fort Pezeries
3 &F.t 1g F.t

New Barracks

+ Torteval
Norwich House
and Battery

Plan mont
Watch House

V.e Watch House
New

1000                    1          2          3000 yards.

T. Hoyd. R.A.R. 6 Bat.n
Fecit.

Map accompanying the
1803 Report.

*Public Records Office*
*Ref. WO 55/1549/11/1*

31

# Critical Report on Towers

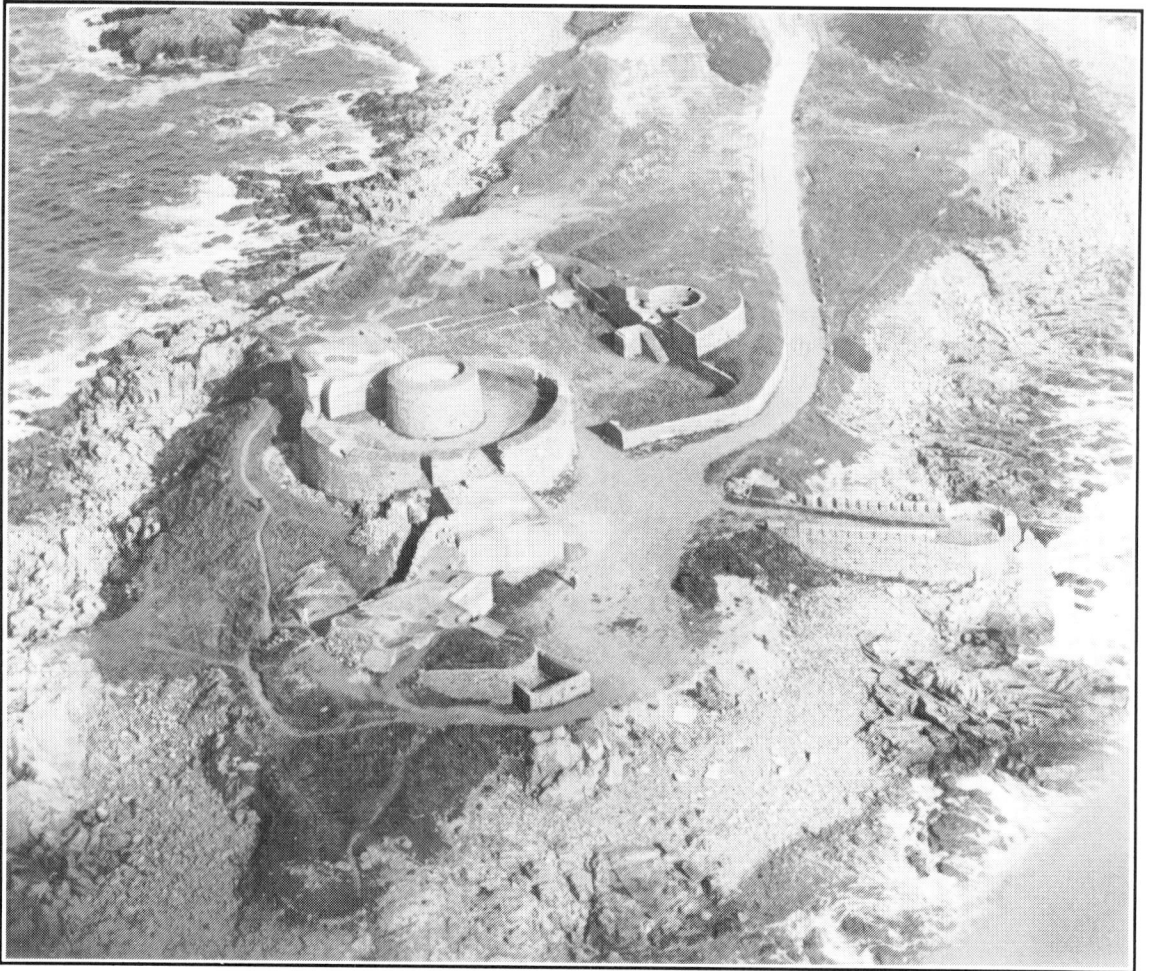

Fort Houmet,
Guernsey,
(1985).

The whole of the Workmanship of the Three Towers is performed in a very careless manner, and it would be very troublesome and expensive to put the Towers into a habitable condition, or to make them fit for military Service. A stick was thrust into the Masonry 18 inc: at Homette Towers.

*Thomas Simon Master Carpenter*
*Mathieu Josterin Master Mason*

Part of a
Critical
Report by
two master
craftsmen.

*Public Records
Office. Ref.
WO 55/808*

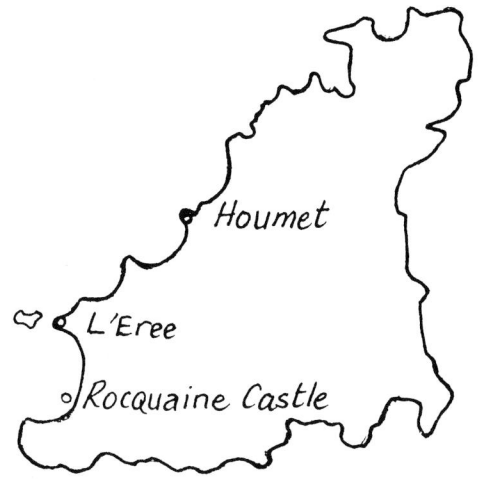

Position of Martello Towers on the west coast of Guernsey.

Following Mackelcan's report, Doyle reported to the War Office on the state of the Island's defences. He stated with reference to Rocquaine Castle that "The part remaining to be done, is first to close the rear of the Battery with a wall of 100 feet in length and about 10 feet medium height . . . . . . and . . . . . . to build a bomb proof casement on the top of the battery."[4] The estimated cost was £500. With reference to L'Eree his report continued, "The original project drawn up by the Commanding Royal Engineer . . . (is) . . . to build a tower in its gorge . . . . . but the States will not consent to build such a tower." Doyle added weight to his recommendations by adding that, "Rear Admiral Sir James Saumarez[5] is so strongly persuaded, that he has repeatedly expressed his approbation (i.e. approval) of the measure I have now the honour to recommend."

It is surprising that when dealing with the defence at the Houmet there was no mention of a tower - only a recommendation to build "a solid battery . . . . . . for about £400," (However, a tower was constructed on this site).

The three towers at Rocquaine, L'Eree and Houmet were started in 1804 under Major General Doyle's orders. Mr. Andrew Gray (Military Draftsman) was appointed as Superintendent of the defence works on the sea line in the island. In the letter[6] appointing him, Superintendent, Andrew Gray was given an allowance to keep a horse because he would lose his extra pay as Military Draftsman.

On the 1st August 1804 the conditions of an agreement between Major General Doyle, (Lieutenant Governor of Guernsey), on behalf of the Government, and Mr. Thomas Henry Junior, (Builder of the Vale Parish) were agreed.[7] The agreement stipulated that the works should be ". . . . . performed in a solid, substantial and workmanlike manner - in default of which Mr. Henry binds himself under a penalty of one thousand pounds to be forfeited to the Government on his being legally convicted of a failure on his part of the service he herein engages to perform." It continued with details of the towers. In particular the agreement stated that Houmet point and L'Eree towers were to be built 25 feet high from the foundations, 20 feet diameter, the walls to be 5.5 feet thick at the bottom and 4.5 feet at the top; the cost being £500. An additional amount of £150 was allowed at L'Eree for the scarping of the rock and enlarging and joining the battery to the tower. The agreement specifically referred to the tower at Rocquaine Castle as a Martello tower, to be built (25 feet diameter) in the centre of the Battery and the walls to be 7 feet thick at the foundation and 6 feet at the top. The works included shutting the work at the gorge by a wall 16 feet high and 6 feet thick, also to making up the wall not less than 16 feet with the rock being scarped down to give the proper height. The amount agreed for the work was £800. In addition to the towers, Mr. Henry was engaged to build six furnaces for heating shot, "The furnaces to be exactly upon the model and of the same dimensions with the one lately built at Mont Crevelt for each of which the said Mr. Henry shall receive

4. P.R.O. W.O. 55/1549.

5. Sir James Saumarez headed the fleet protecting the Channel Islands.

6. Lieutenant Governor's Letter book I, 1.8.1804 (Greffe) Page 84. A letter from Lieutenant Governor, Major General Doyle appointing Mr. Andrew Gray as superintendent.

7. Greffe:- Lieutenant Governor's Letter book I, Pages 89, 90, 91. Agreement re-building Martello Towers, 1.8.1804.

# Request for Fitting Out of Martello Tower

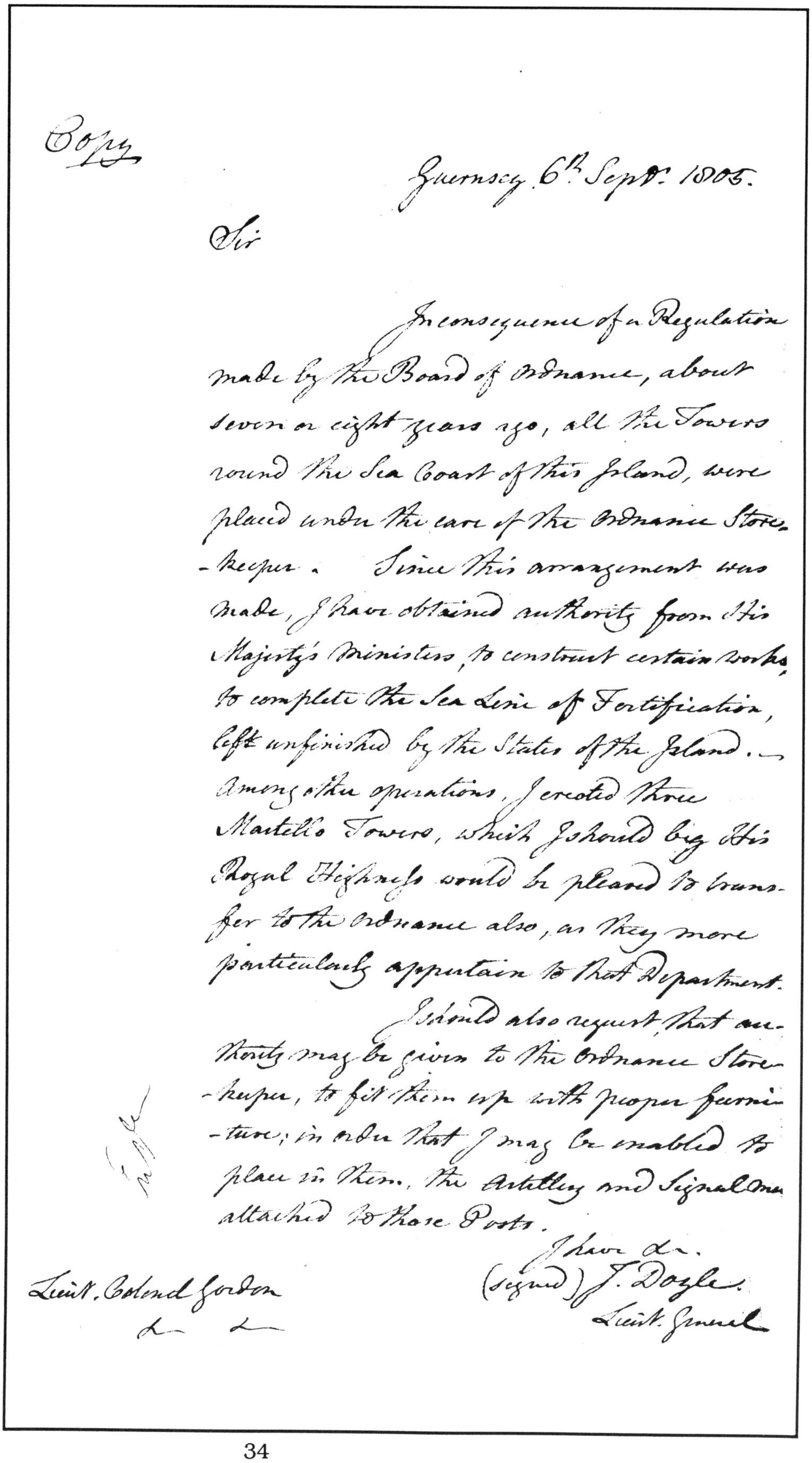

A Letter from
Lieut. General J. Doyle.
6th September, 1805,
Guernsey.
*P.R.O. WO 55/808*

Copy

Guernsey 6th Sept. 1805.

Sir

In consequence of a Regulation made by the Board of Ordnance, about seven or eight years ago, all the Towers round the Sea Coast of this Island, were placed under the care of the Ordnance Store-keeper. Since this arrangement was made, I have obtained authority from His Majesty's Ministers, to construct certain works, to complete the Sea Line of Fortification, left unfinished by the States of the Island. Among other operations, I erected three Martello Towers, which I should beg His Royal Highness would be pleased to transfer to the Ordnance also, as they more particularly appertain to that Department.

I should also request, that authority may be given to the Ordnance Store-keeper, to fit them up with proper furniture; in order that I may be enabled to place in them, the Artillery and Signal Men attached to those Posts.

I have &c.

(signed) J. Doyle.

Lieut. General

Lieut. Colonel Gordon

thirty pounds. In order to enable the said Mr. Henry to execute the foregoing works at this reduced estimate, Government engaged to furnish the said Thomas Henry with as may soldiers to serve as labourers, and such masons, bricklayers, and quarrymen as may be found among the troops of the garrison and are not already employed in the public departments, at the regulated military allowance for working pay. . . . . Major General Doyle engages to supply the said Thomas Henry with tools scaffolding and powder to be used by the miners and Quarrymen in blowing the rocks." It is clear that the work was contracted as cheaply as possible and the penalty clause was a Government safeguard.

In a private letter[8] to Lieutenant General Morse, (Inspector General), from the Commander Royal Engineers Mackelcan reported in 1805 that the three towers "were not yet finished, as the men complain of their uncomfortable residence, (and) the rain comes through their tops. They have been erected by very indifferent workmen, and one of them the largest at Rocquaine fell down as soon as the arch was turned." His comments on the construction were critical in the extreme. "Each of these Towers is mounted with a carronade but Major Wicks, Comd. of the Artillery says they will fall down at the firing of them; he complains also of the furnaces and magazines endangering the blowing up of the men." One reason for the Engineers not building the tower was the cost, for Mackelcan states in his letter that "The whole workmanship was hurried on at the cheapest possible rate as Mr. Gray (Military Architect) seems to have persuaded General Doyle that he could do what Engineers were incapable of doing." Obviously minimizing the cost of building the towers was of paramount importance for the cost of building a tower was reported to be £2,000 - £3,000 in England compared with £500 in Guernsey although the specifications were not identical. In the same letter Mackelcan wrote, "Mr. Gray seems to have persuaded the General that his Towers are quite as good as those which Engineers build altho' they don't cost half so much." He was concerned that the engineers would have to put them to rights later. He continued his letter by stating that the buildings were only suitable for barracks. "My opinion, however is, that as these Towers have the character of barracks or should be considered as such (as they are to be garrisoned by ten or twenty men . . .)" and concluded his letter by saying that if plans and sections of the Towers were required he would need the "favour of a draftsman".

Just a few days later Mackelcan wrote a second private letter[9] to General Morse, "I visited the towers with two of our Master Artificers who made out the enclosed report . . . . . I have no hestitation in adding my testimony." The report was compiled by Thomas Simon, (Master Carpenter) and Mathieu Tostevin, (Master Mason). Their joint opinion was that "The whole of the workmanship of the three towers, is performed in a very careless manner, and it would be very troublesome and expensive to put the Towers into a habitable

8. P.R.O. 55/808 24th September 1805.

9. P.R.O. W.O. 55/808 Letter to General Morse 28th September 1805.

35

# Inspection
# Order

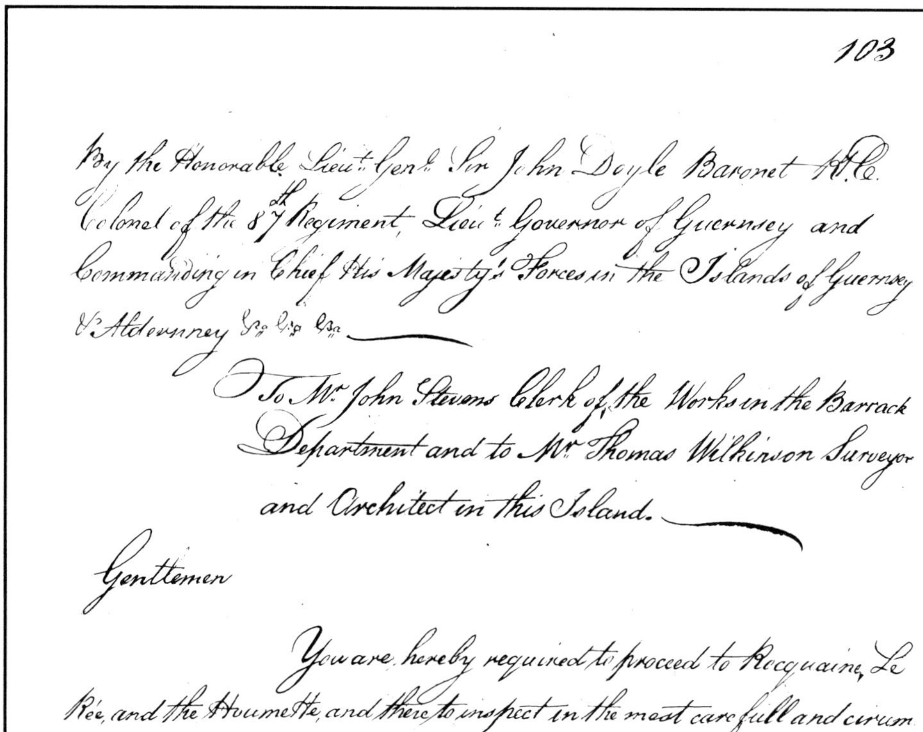

Directive from
Lieut. Governor Doyle to
John Stevens,
Clerk of Works, and
Thomas Wilkinson,
Surveyor and Architect, to
inspect the Martello Towers
at Rocquaine, L'Eree, and
Houmette, Guernsey.
23rd October, 1805.

*By Permission of the Greffe, Guernsey.*
*Letter Book of Lieut. Governor*
*1804-1805.*
*Page 103.*

103

By the Honorable Lieut. Genl. Sir John Doyle Baronet K.C.
Colonel of the 87th Regiment, Lieut. Governor of Guernsey and
Commanding in Chief His Majesty's Forces in the Islands of Guernsey
& Alderenney &c &c &c.

To Mr. John Stevens Clerk of the Works in the Barrack
Department and to Mr. Thomas Wilkinson Surveyor
and Architect in this Island.

Gentlemen

You are hereby required to proceed to Rocquaine, Le
Rée, and the Houmette, and there to inspect in the most carefull and circum
stantial manner the Martello Towers built at those posts — You will
also take with you such other professional persons as you may think
proper the better to enable you to form a correct judgement on the subjects
in question ——— You will be particular and minute in your
examination as it may be requisite to verify the same upon Oath:—
You will Report your Opinion as to the Workmanship and Materials
of the Towers in question, and, Observe if there are any Rents or Settlements in the Walls, that indicate a want of Strength or Solidity —

Given at Government House
Guernsey 23rd October 1805

(Signed) Doyle Lt. General
Commandg.

condition, or to make them fit for military service." The report also detailed the sizes and commented on the state of the masonry.

Commenting on the Rocquaine Tower, Simon and Tostevin reported[10] "That the masonry is badly executed and in some places without mortar. A stick was pushed into the wall in two or three places 15 inches deep." They criticized the provision for musketry "The banquet . . . for musquetry (is) . . . only 13 inches broad and too low for men to fire over . . .The top of the arch is plastered with unslacked lime, and broken in many places. It is impossible to keep out the rain with such a finish." They also questioned the suitability of the room to be used as a powder magazine as it had" . . .no door . . . and no air holes." Lastly they said "The powder magazine which contains all the Ordnance Stores for this battery, is upon the rocks without the walls of the battery . . . . . . so that is will continue to be a very insecure place for powder until something further be done".

The report on L'Eree tower also refers to shoddy workmanship "The plastering etc. on the top of the tower (is) as bad as at Rocquaine . . . . . .The soldiers complain of the dampness of the walls, and the darkness of the room, as there is no light when the door is shut . . . . The cellar story (sic) is not finished . . . . . and (there are) no air holes, though it is said to be for a Powder magazine." This tower was mounted with a 24 pr. carronade at the time of the inspection.

Similar criticisms also appear concerning the workmanship on the Homette (Houmet) tower."The Gunner complains that rats come in under the foundations. . . . . The door is made all awry . . . . The masonry as bad as at Rocquaine . . . . The principle floor . . . . . . is plastered but the plastering is not dry. It is reported that the mortar was in part made with salt water . . . . A stick was thrust into the masonry 18 inches at Homette Tower." The Houmet tower was mounted with a 24 pr. carronade at the time and the only complimentary remark in the report stated that it was "better made for musketry defence."

The report concluded by saying "The whole of the workmanship of the three Towers, is performed in a very careless manner and it would be very troublesome and expensive to put the towers into a habitable condition, or make them fit for military service."

It would seem that pressure was brought to bear on Major General Doyle to have an independent report on the state of the towers, and to evaluate the workmanship and materials because of the penalty clause in the contract. On the 23rd October, 1805, General Doyle instructed Mr. John Stevens, Clerk of the Works in the Barracks Department, and Mr. Thomas Wilkinson, Surveyor and Architect (in Guernsey), to inspect the three Martello towers at the sites and report back to him:-

*"Gentlemen,*
*You are hereby required to proceed to Rocquaine, Le Ree and the Houmette, and there to inspect in the most careful and circumstantial manner the Martello Towers built at those posts- You will also take with you such other professional persons as you may think proper, the better*

10. P.R.O. W.O. 55/808 Report 28th September 1805 by Thomas Simon and Mathieu Tostevin. (See page 32).

# Fort
# Saumarez

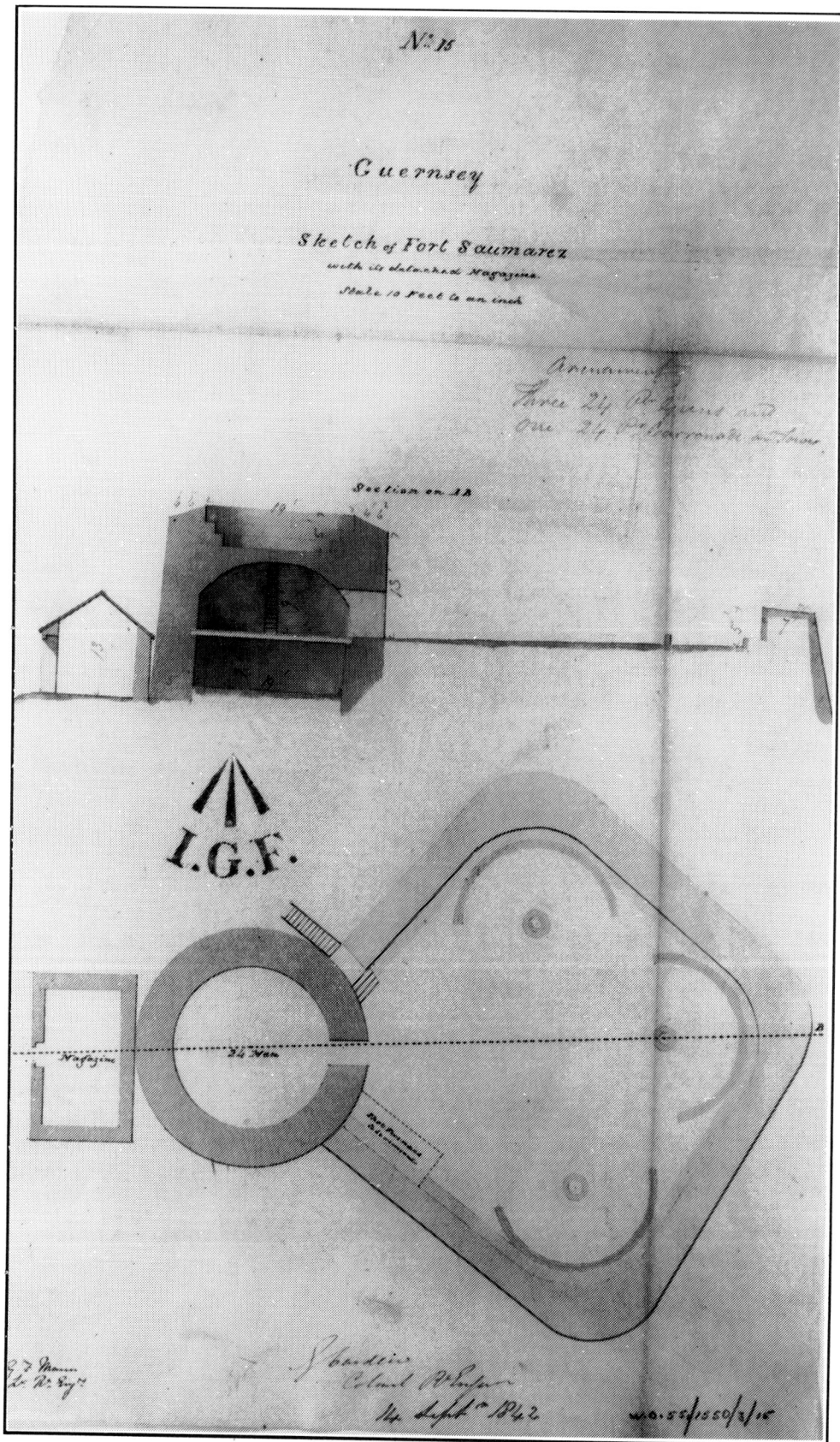

Sketch of Fort Saumarez
showing its detached
magazine.

*to enable you to form a correct judgement on the subjects in question-
You will be particular and minute in your examination as it may be
requisite to verify the same upon Oath. You will report your opinion as
to the workmanship and materials of the tower in question, and
observe if there are any rents or settlements in the walls that indicate a
want of strength or solidity. Given at Government House, Guernsey,
23rd October, 1805. Signed J. Doyle, Lt. General, Commander."* [11]

The following day Stevens and Wilkinson replied to Doyle's letter
informing him that Mr. Robert Goodwin, (Carpenter and Builder) and
Mr. William Ball, (Master Mason), would assist them with the
examination of the three Martello Towers.[12] Messrs. Stevens,
Wilkinson, Goodwin and Ball reported back on the 25th October,
1805, and before Eleazer Le Marchant, (Bailiff) and in the presence of
John Carey and John Tupper, (Jurats of the Royal Court), under oath
said that they "were of the opinion that the materials are good, that the
workmanship is executed in a strong and substantial manner and that
there are no rents or settlements of any kind that indicate a want of
strength or solidity."[13] There were obviously discrepancies between the
official and the unofficial reports but no action seems to have been
taken.

## BRAYE DU VALLE

The Island of Guernsey was once made up of two islands separated
by a channel from Grand Havre eastwards to St. Sampson's harbour
and this is shown clearly on the 1680 Legge Report. The Braye was by
no means only a narrow channel. It was of irregular width with much
of it submerged twice daily by the rising tide to a depth of eight to
twelve feet. For a number of years Grand Havre was considered a
weakness in the island's defences. Mackelcan's Report recommended
mooring vessels across the bay or making a dyke to make the area more
secure.[14] The navy also considered the Braye vulnerable. In a letter,
Admiral Sir James Saumarez summed up the situation in the following
way: "I have my great satisfaction in acquainting your lordship, that the
works which have been granted to me by the States, are carrying on
with an alacrity never before witnessed in Guernsey heretofore
proverbial for its slowness in all public measures; and that the greatest
harmony and good humour prevails between the inhabitants and the
government in this Island, I am not without sanguine hopes of
obtaining from the States, the important object of forming a pier at the
entrance of St. Sampson's Harbour; which will not only considerably
strengthen and secure the North East part of the island, but give a
prodigious increase to its commerce; and ultimately will aid and
forward my proposal, for recovering the submerged land of the Brae
du Valle, thereby restoring near 300 acres to the cultivation of the
Island . . . ."[15]. It should be noted that at the St. Sampson's end of the
channel [16] a chaussee protected the entrance.

*11. Greffe: Lieutenant Governor Letter
book I, 1803-1805, Page 103, 23rd
October 1805. (See page 36).*

*12. Greffe: Lieutenant Governor Letter
book I, 1803-1805, Page 104, 24th
October 1805.*

*13. Greffe: Lieutenant Governor Letter
book 1803-1805, Page 105.*

*14. P.R.O. W.O. 30/57 Report 1803
29th August 1803.*

*15. P.R.O. W.O. 1/605 Letter from
Admiral Sir James Saumarez 13th
September, 1803.*

*16. Greffe: Book 2 Lieutenant
Governor's book Doyle 1803.*

# Braye
# du
# Valle

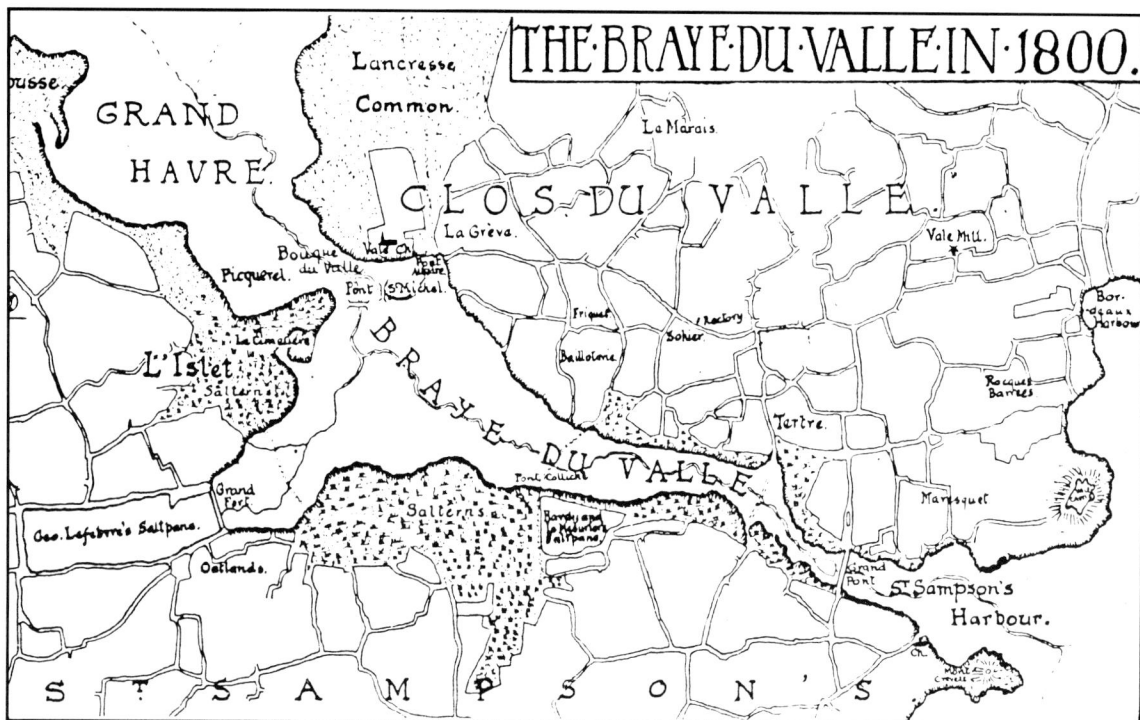

THE·BRAYE·DU·VALLE·IN·1800.

Société
Guernesiaise
Vol. XII 1935
Paper by
Major
S. C. Curtis

Grand Havre,
1986.
*(Rousse Tower
on the Left
hand side)*

Major General Doyle was responsible for the reclamation of the Braye because he feared that if an enemy landed on the North of the island he would not be able to reinforce his troops because of the salt water channel. He convinced the Government that the reclamation of the Braye was essential for securing and retaining the island, and in March 1806 he inserted a notice in 'La Gazette de Guernesey'[17] asking for tenders for the construction of a dam across St. Sampson's harbour and another westward of the Vale Church to shut out the sea which overflowed the land. The work had to be solid and permanent, and to include sluices at the west end as well as at the east end and included the keeping of the sluices and dams in good condition for seven years.[18]

Thomas Henry[19] was contracted to build the embankments and sluices in May 1806 and completed them in one year. Labourers were employed from among the inhabitants as well as soldiers with the sergeants acting as overseers. The land was sold in 1808. An announcement in the 'Gazette' stated that the land which had been reclaimed would be sold to the highest bidder with the exception of a piece which would be retained for the drilling of troops, - or else in lots of 50 vergees[20] each. Offers for each parcel of land had to be sent to Government House. The 300 acres of land realised £5,000 which Doyle gave to the States of Guernsey for building roads. One such road named "Route Militaire" was built across the reclaimed land so soldiers could move more quickly to support the towers and batteries in the North of the Island. Two other roads were also built from St. Peter Port, one to L'Eree and the other to Vazon for the same reason of reinforcing the towers and batteries as quickly as possible. These roads are referred to in Berry's History of Guernsey, published in 1815, as "Doyle's Military Roads."

17. La Gazette de Guernesey March 1806.

18. Societe Guernesiaise Vol. XII 1935 The Braye du Valle paper by Major S. C. Curtis.

19. The same person who built the towers on the west coast.

20. Vergee - Is a Guernsey measurement of land 1 acre = 2.5 vergee approximately.

# Jersey
# Towers

Plan of Lewis Tower,
St. Ouen's Bay.

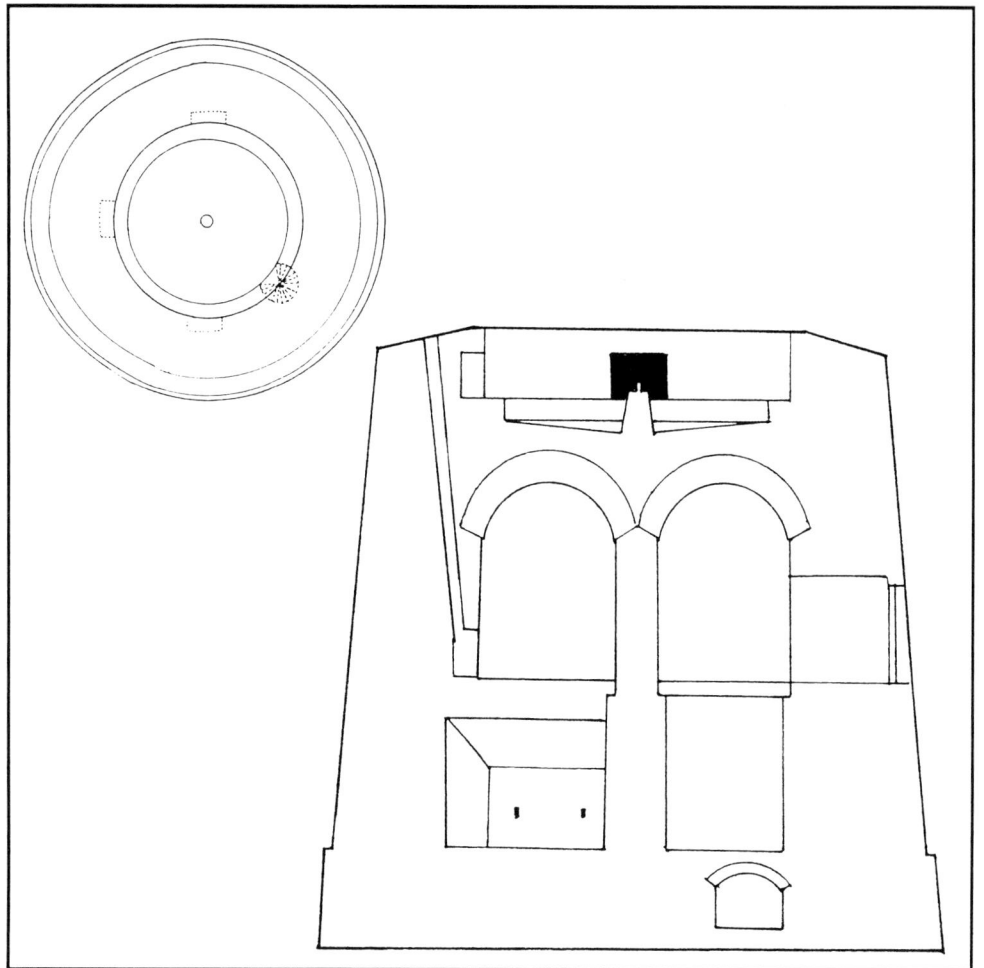

Plan of Kempt Tower,
St. Ouen's, Jersey.

Photograph of Jersey Tower

# Chapter 4
# Jersey Martello Towers

As previously explained in chapter two[1], the early towers (pre-Martello) were suggested by General Conway, resident Governor of Jersey (1772 - 1795). Originally thirty towers were proposed, in July 1778, to be built around the coastline of Jersey. There were numerous delays and only twenty three towers[2] were finally built. The last tower completed in this style was at La Rocco (1798). I believe these towers were built without machicoules initially, (as described in chapter five[3]), and they were only added when it was realised that a safe area was created under the loop holes at the base of the tower[4]. These towers were designed solely for muskets to be fired from the loopholes and roof.

Between 1807 and 1814 a further three Martello towers were added and these bear a close resemblence to the English south coast towers. These towers were built with a larger base, a steeper batter, but were not so high as the pre-martello towers and were also void of loop holes. They were built solely for mounting a carronade on the roof and the tower was used for stores and accommodation for the artillery men manning the guns.

The last group of Martello towers to be built in Europe were begun in Jersey in 1834, having been planned two years earlier. There were five towers built and not surprisingly they have some of the characteristics of the English east coast Martello towers.

Lewis Tower was built with an elliptical base with the thicker wall towards the sea. It has a central pillar and a circular spiral staircase between the floors.

L'Etac tower was built like the south coast tower and had a resemblance to Noirmont tower built in 1814. This tower had an arch and no central pillar.

Kempt tower was built in a substantial manner, being cam shaped at the base with a trifoil gun platform (a feature seen in east coast towers). This tower also had the thicker wall towards the sea side.

1. Page 17.

2. Twenty two round towers and Seymour tower (the only tower built square)

3. Page 47.

4. P.R.O. WO 30/57 Defence of the Channel Islands page 47, 48, 25th November 1802. Major John Humfrey, Royal Engineers.

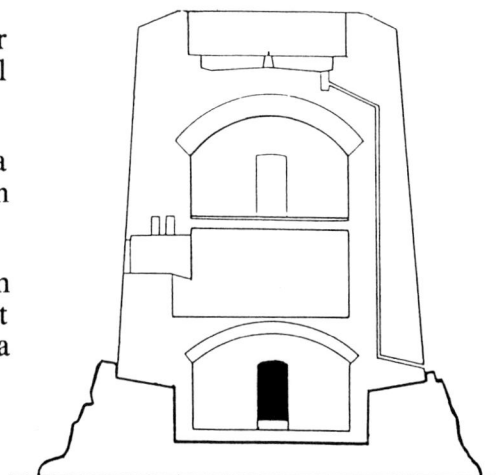
Noirmont Tower, 1814

# Map of
# Jersey

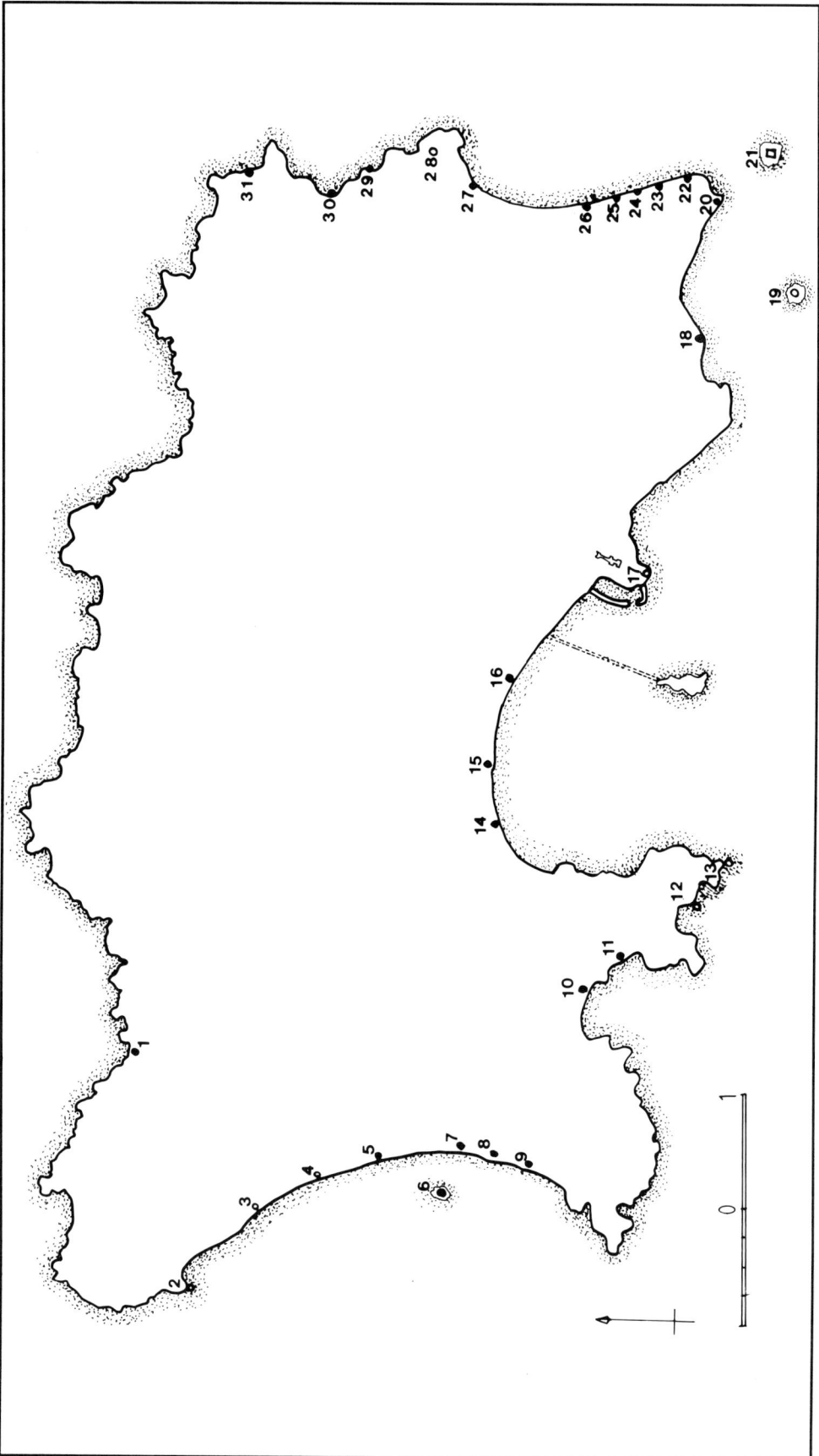

Map of Jersey indicating
where the towers of Jersey
are situated.

44

# Jersey Towers

| | Towers Name | Date Built | *Still standing |
|---|---|---|---|
| 1 | GREVE DE LECQ | Sept. 1780 | * |
| 5 | ST. OUEN No. 3 or | | Germans destroyed |
| | D (Hightower) | – | in World War II |
| 6 | LA ROCCO | 1796-98 | * |
| 7 | ST. OUEN C. | – | Destroyed |
| 8 | ST. OUEN B | – | Destroyed |
| 9 | ST. OUEN A. | – | Destroyed by sea/ completed by artillery |
| 10 | ST. BRELADE No. 2 | – | * |
| 11 | ST. BRELADE No. 1 | – | * |
| 12 | PORTELET | 1807-08 | * |
| 13 | NOIRMONT | 1808-14 | * |
| 14 | THIRD TOWER (Beaumont) | – | * |
| 15 | SECOND TOWER | – | Germans destroyed in World War II |
| 16 | FIRST TOWER | – | * |
| 18 | LE HOCQ | – | * |
| 19 | ICHO | 1811 | * |
| 20 | PLAT ROCQUE | 1781 | * |
| 21 | SEYMOUR (only Square Tower) | 1781 | * |
| 22 | GROUVILLE No. 1 (La Rocque) | – | * |
| 23 | GROUVILLE No. 2 (Keppel Tower) | – | * |
| 24 | GROUVILLE No. 3 | – | * |
| 25 | GROUVILLE No. 4 | – | * |
| 26 | GROUVILLE No. 5 | – | * |
| 27 | GROUVILLE NO. 6 | – | Destroyed possibly to build Gorey Village Railway Station. |
| 29 | ARCHIRONDEL | 1793-94 | * |
| 30 | ST. CATHERINES | – | * |
| 31 | FLIQUET (Telegraph Tower) | – | * |

## LAST GROUP OF MARTELLO TOWERS BUILT IN EUROPE

| | | | |
|---|---|---|---|
| 2 | L'ETACQ | 1834 | Germans destroyed in World War II |
| 3 | LEWIS | 1835 | * |
| 4 | KEMPT | 1834-38 | * |
| 17 | LA COLETTE | 1834 | * |
| 28 | VICTORIA | 1837 | * |

List of Jersey Towers numbered for use with the Map opposite.

# Early
# Towers

Guernsey
Early
Towers
1778

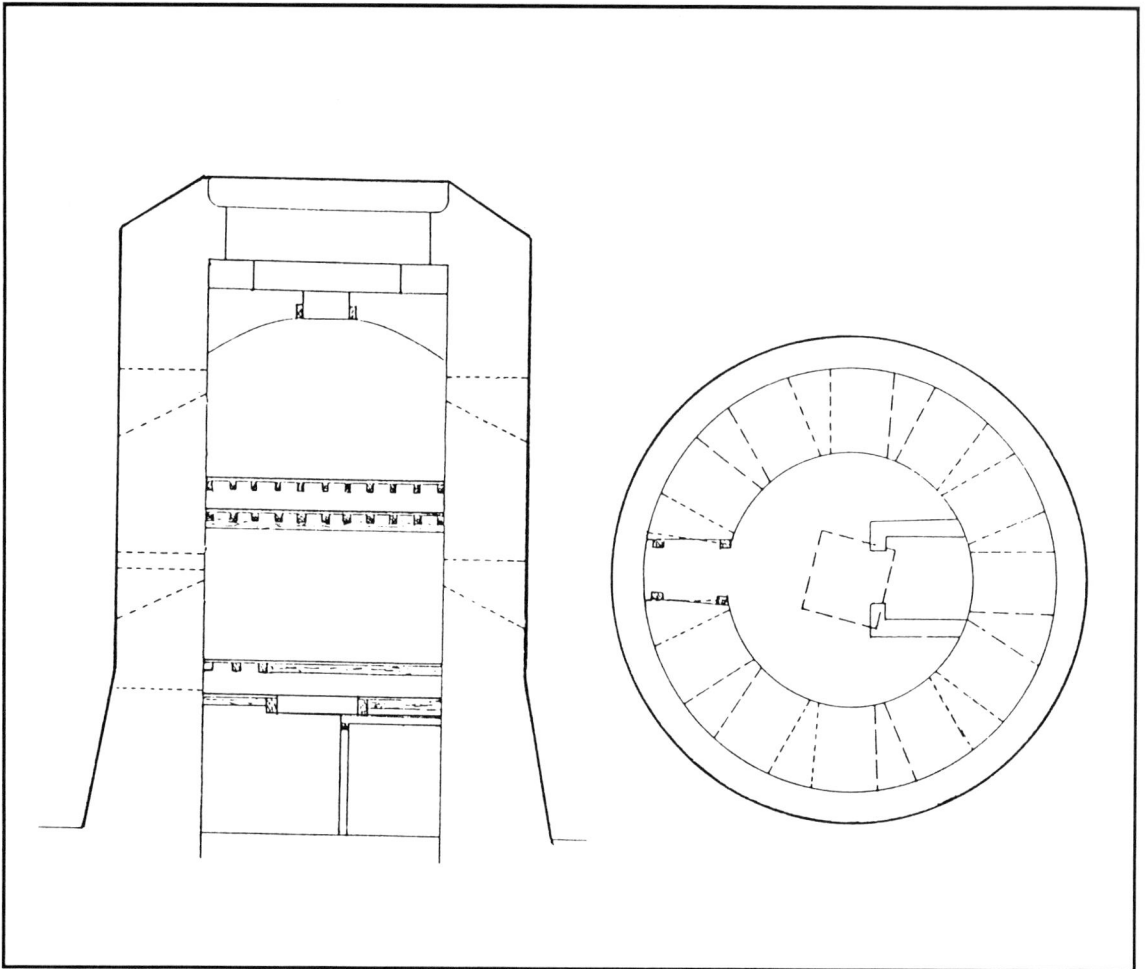

Jersey
Early
Towers
1778

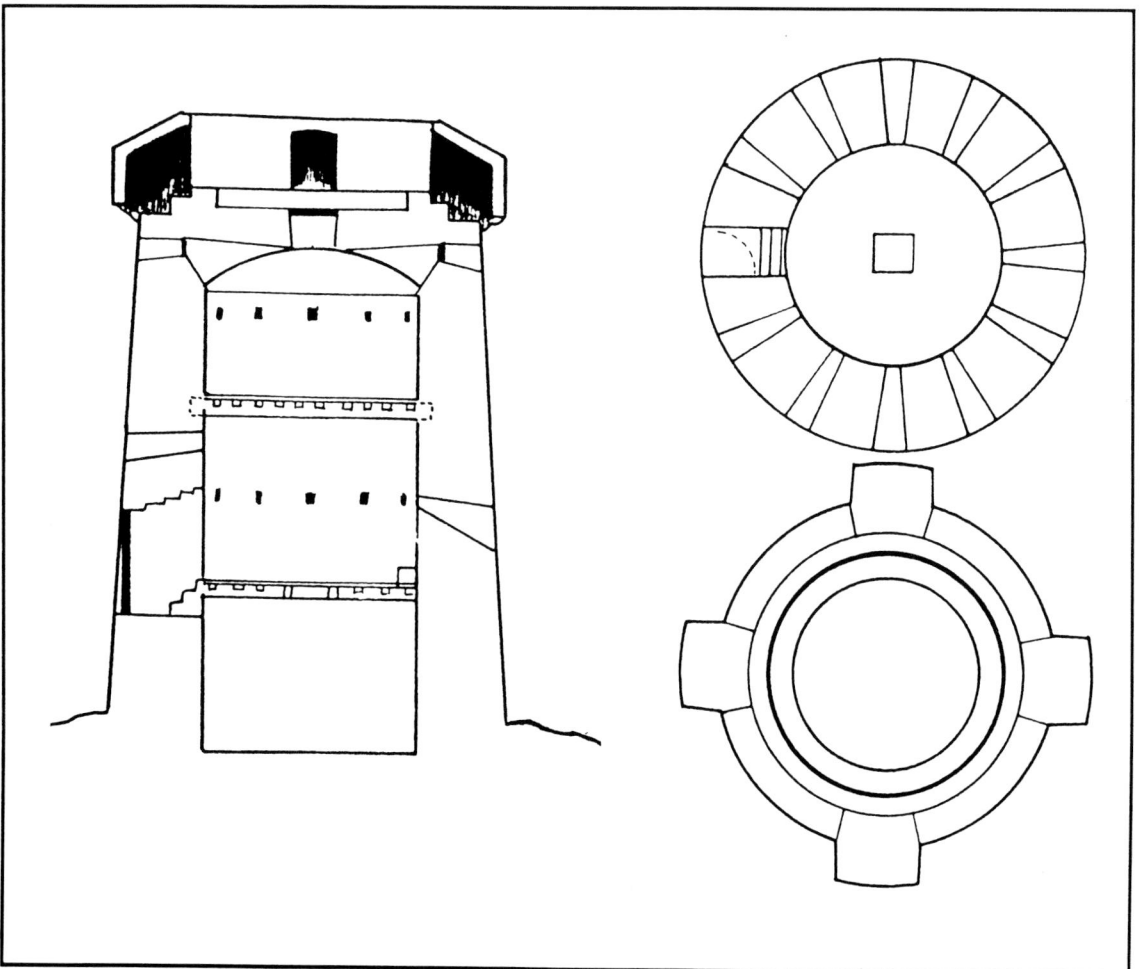

# Chapter 5
# Comparative Study

Jersey - Guernsey 1778
Guernsey - England - Jersey
1804-1837.
Martello Towers Proposed
but not Built.
Last Tower Built in Guernsey
1856.

## PRE-MARTELLO TOWER DESIGN

The reason for building the towers was to defend the beaches. They were designed specifically for musket fire because of the shortage of cannon. It was not until 1803 that General Doyle successfully mounted carronades on the roofs of the Guernsey towers[1] after recommendation from Mackelcan's report that 18 pound carronades be mounted in 1802.

1. P.R.O. W.O. 1/605, 11th August 1803 Letter from General Doyle stating he intended to mount carronades on top of the towers.

## PRE-MARTELLO TOWER CONSTRUCTION AND MATERIALS USED

The construction of the towers in both Guernsey and Jersey began about the same time - in August 1778 - but the Guernsey Towers progressed at a faster rate and were finished in 1779. The building of the Jersey towers was hampered by labour problems. Their 22 towers were not completed until 1794. From my research it would appear that these towers were built independently, although the same Officer, Captain Bassett, was initially involved with the building in both islands. Consequently, it cannot be claimed that the designs being used in each island were not known in the other.

N.B. 23 Towers were built including Seymour which was square.

Why the towers differ in size is not known. No reason has so far been postulated or plan found to shed light on this mystery. Some of the Jersey towers were originally built without machicoules, because in 1802 a report stated "Few of them have machicoules, for want of which, a space of Thirty feet round each tower is not seen."[2] (The musket firing (depression) angle being so acute that a 'safe area' was created for an invader under the wall. This had been a problem in Norman castles and was solved by creating machicoules to fire down the walls on the enemy). It would therefore seem that these were not incorporated in the original towers, but were later added when this problem became apparent.

2. P.R.O. W.O. 30/57 Mackelcans report 25th November 1802. The report proposed mounting carronades and that four small machicoules be added.

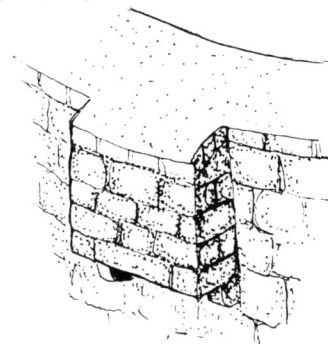

Machicoule used on Jersey Towers.

These early towers were built out of the local granite. The walls of the Jersey towers were thicker and the walls had a slight batter (taper), whereas, the Guernsey towers are parellel and only sloped outwards in the lower third of the wall. The entrances are well off the ground and were entered by means of a ladder. Ladders were also used to reach the other floors and basement once inside the towers. The internal floors were made of wood with trap doors to the next floor. A firing step was built out of timber 15-18 inches high continuously around the wall with

# Jersey
# Tower

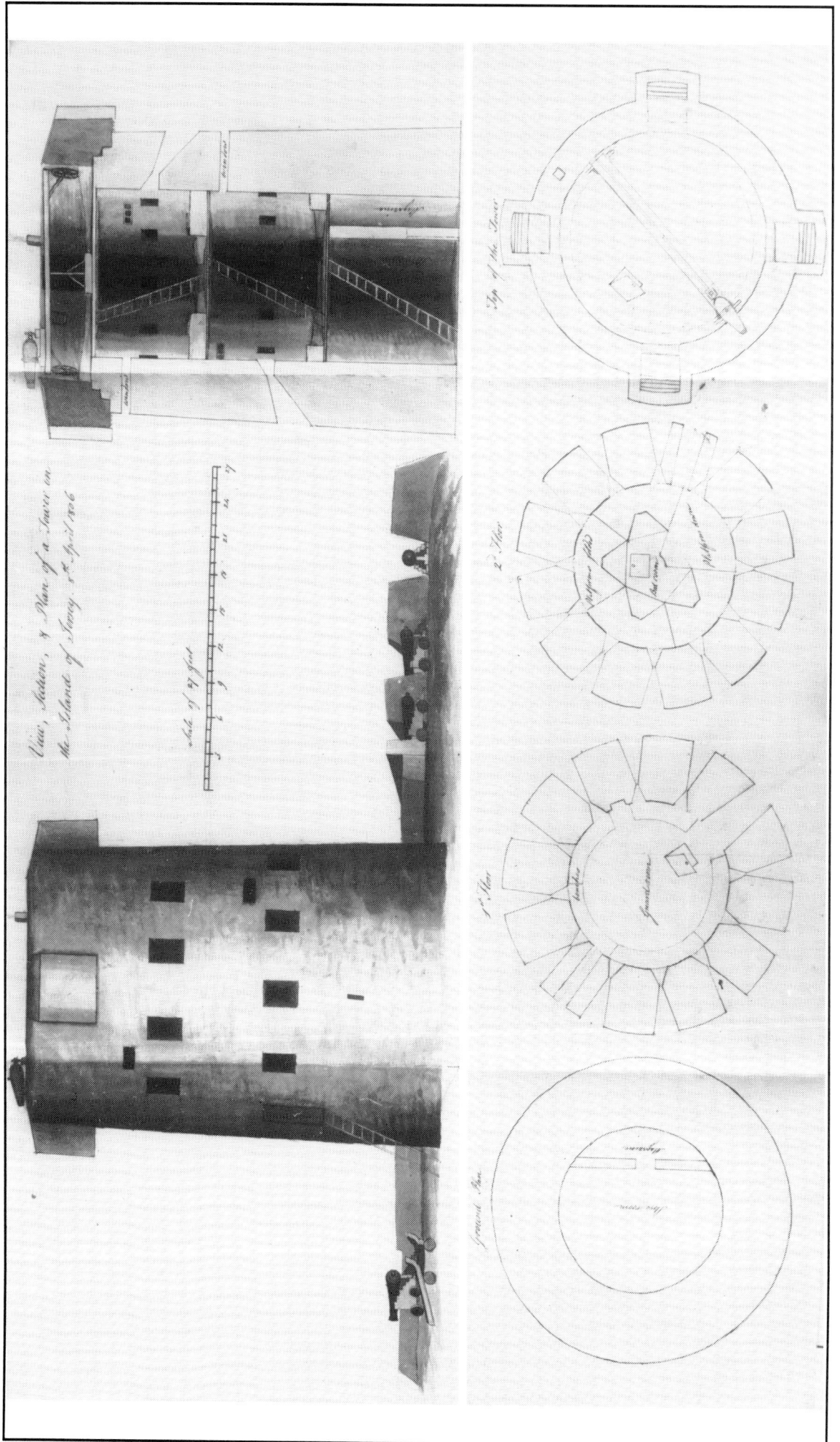

View, Section,
and Plan of
Jersey Tower,
1806.

*Public Records Office
Ref. WO 30/77*

a break for the door and fireplace. An elevation of the Jersey tower drawn in 1806 shows the second floor divided into five segments and flaps hinged to form a false floor[3]. Whether this was original or a later modification is difficult to tell; but it was possibly used for sleeping on.

3. See page opposite.

Bricks were used in the construction of the vaulting in both Guernsey and Jersey towers, and also for the fireplaces and dividing the basement for stores. It was proposed in 1792 to vault the first floor of the Guernsey towers with bricks in place of the wood, but I have not seen any tower modified in this way, and therefore presume it was not carried out. A Guernsey tower required more than 2,000 bricks in its construction, and a quick calculation suggests that a Jersey tower probably required twice this number.

The pre-Martello towers in Jersey and Guernsey lack one basic, and essential quality, a capacity to be used for artillery, and, for this reason, cannot be called true "Martello Towers" in their original form. Later a carronade was mounted on the top of these towers in both Guernsey and Jersey. Over the years the term "Martello" has been used to identify any coastal tower, and not just the towers built during the Napoleonic wars.

# COMPARISON BETWEEN GUERNSEY, ENGLISH AND JERSEY TOWERS

## MARTELLO TOWERS 1804 - 1812

Two Guernsey towers were proposed in 1803:-

### L'EREE - FORT SAUMAREZ

Lieutenant Colonel Mackelcan, reporting on the defence works at L'Eree, stated that " . . . . . . a small tower (is) proposed to be erected for the accommodation of eighteen men (being) the number requisite to work the three guns. The Tower should be provided with water, meat and bread for ten days and ammunition to the amount of 100 rounds a gun and 2000 rounds of ball cartridges. A carronade should be mounted on the top of the Tower when finished. . . . . The defendants may hold the Tower for several days as it is not likely the enemy will deem it worthwhile to beseige it in his way to Fort George."[4] Three towers were built the following year so it would seem that the idea of towers was accepted at a time when agreement could not be reached on the English towers. It is possible that the earlier coastal towers already built in the Channel Islands set a precedent and therefore made it easy for General Doyle to build these later models. The budget for the Guernsey towers was considerably lower than for the English towers.[5] There are

4. P.R.O. W.O. 55/1547 Report on defence works, Lieutenant Colonel Mackelcan 1803.

5. Guernsey Towers cost £500. English Towers £3,000-£5,000.

# Comparison Chart

*A comparison between Channel Island and English Towers.*

## Specification of CHANNEL ISLES Towers Compared with ENGLISH Martello Towers

| Tower | Height | Diameter base | Diameter top | Wall thickness base | Wall thickness top | Wall thickness seaside | Construction brick | Construction granite | Sloping walls | Number built |
|---|---|---|---|---|---|---|---|---|---|---|
| **ENGLAND** | | | | | | | | | | |
| ESSEX 1808 | | | | | | | ✓ | – | ✓ | 29 |
| SUSSEX KENT 1805 | | | | | | | ✓ | – | ✓ | 74 |
| TOWER 59 (PEVENSEY) | 30' | 40' | | 9'6" | | | ✓ | – | ✓ | |
| TOWER 73 (WISH TOWER) | | | | | 5' | 11' | ✓ | – | ✓ | |
| **JERSEY** | | | | | | | | | | |
| KEMPT 1834 | 34' | 60' | | 10' | 7' | | ✓ | ✓ | ✓ | 1 |
| LEWIS 1835 | 32' | 38' | 34' | 9' | 7' | | ✓ | ✓ | ✓ | 1 |
| L'ETAC 1810 | 34' | 32' | 28' | 8' | 6' | | ✓ | ✓ | ✓ | 1 |
| NORMONT 1778 | 30' | 32' | | 7'6" | 5' | | ✓ | ✓ | ✓ | 1 |
| EARLY TOWERS 1778 | 36' | 34' | | 8' | 6' | | ✓ | ✓ | ✓ | 21 |
| **GUERNSEY** | | | | | | | | | | |
| HOMMET & SAUMAREZ | 25' | 20' | | 7' | 5'6" | | ✓ | ✓ | ✓ | 2 |
| FORT GREY 1804 | 26' | 37' | | 7' | 4'6" | | ✓ | ✓ | ✓ | 1 |
| EARLY TOWERS 1778 | 30' | 20' | | 4' | 6' | | ✓ | ✓ | ✗ | 15 |

two possible reasons for this: Firstly the Guernsey towers were built from granite, which was quarried locally and therefore the transport costs were less. Secondly the towers were smaller [6] and therefore there would be a reduction in building time (lower wage bills) and less material to be used. The English towers, on the other hand, built in 1805, were principally built from bricks. Not only would they take longer to build, but they would also require materials to be transported over greater distances.

6. Refer to Specification chart opposite re sizes of towers.

Only the towers at Rocquaine and Houmet (Guernsey) were built inside a perimeter wall whereas the larger English towers had a dry ditch around them. The smaller towers were built 400-500 yards apart and close to the beach. This in time was to prove disastrous as the sea undermined their foundations. Fort Saumarez in Guernsey had a battery adjoining it, a feature that can be seen in the Jersey towers.

The Jersey towers that were built in 1811 are very close in specification to the English towers. This is not surprising as the experience gained in England would have been applied to later designs because the Ordnance Department would have had to be consulted. The Jersey towers were built from granite, as were their Guernsey cousins, and only later were they stuccoed to try to prevent damp, whereas all the English towers had stucco applied over the brickwork during construction. (Noirmont Tower in Jersey may have been built with a smaller diameter because it was built on a rock which limited the area of the base but it still has the characteristics of the English towers - a tapered flowerpot appearance.)

The buildings were entered on the first floor by ladder and once inside a stone spiral staircase led to each floor. A ladder was used to reach the basement in some towers, whereas the Guernsey towers used ladders to reach each floor. At Houmet Tower the basement was reached by going down stairs outside the tower but inside the perimeter wall. All the towers had carronades mounted on their tops on traversing platforms.

A Martello Tower near Hythe, split in half by the sea. (*Photograph from King & His Army and Navy News, Vol. 16*).

# MARTELLO TOWERS 1812 - 1837

Early Pre-Martello towers in Guernsey were built concentrically whereas later towers in England (1808) were built with an elliptical base with the thickest part facing the sea. Kempt Tower in Jersey was built with an elliptical base in 1837 and bears a close resemblance to the England east coast towers. It is interesting to note that Jersey was the last place in Britain where Martello towers were built. [7] Between 1832-1837 three further towers were built in Jersey and all of them show the advancement in the building of Martellos.

7. Square gun towers were built but do not have the same characteristics.

# Fort
# Pembroke

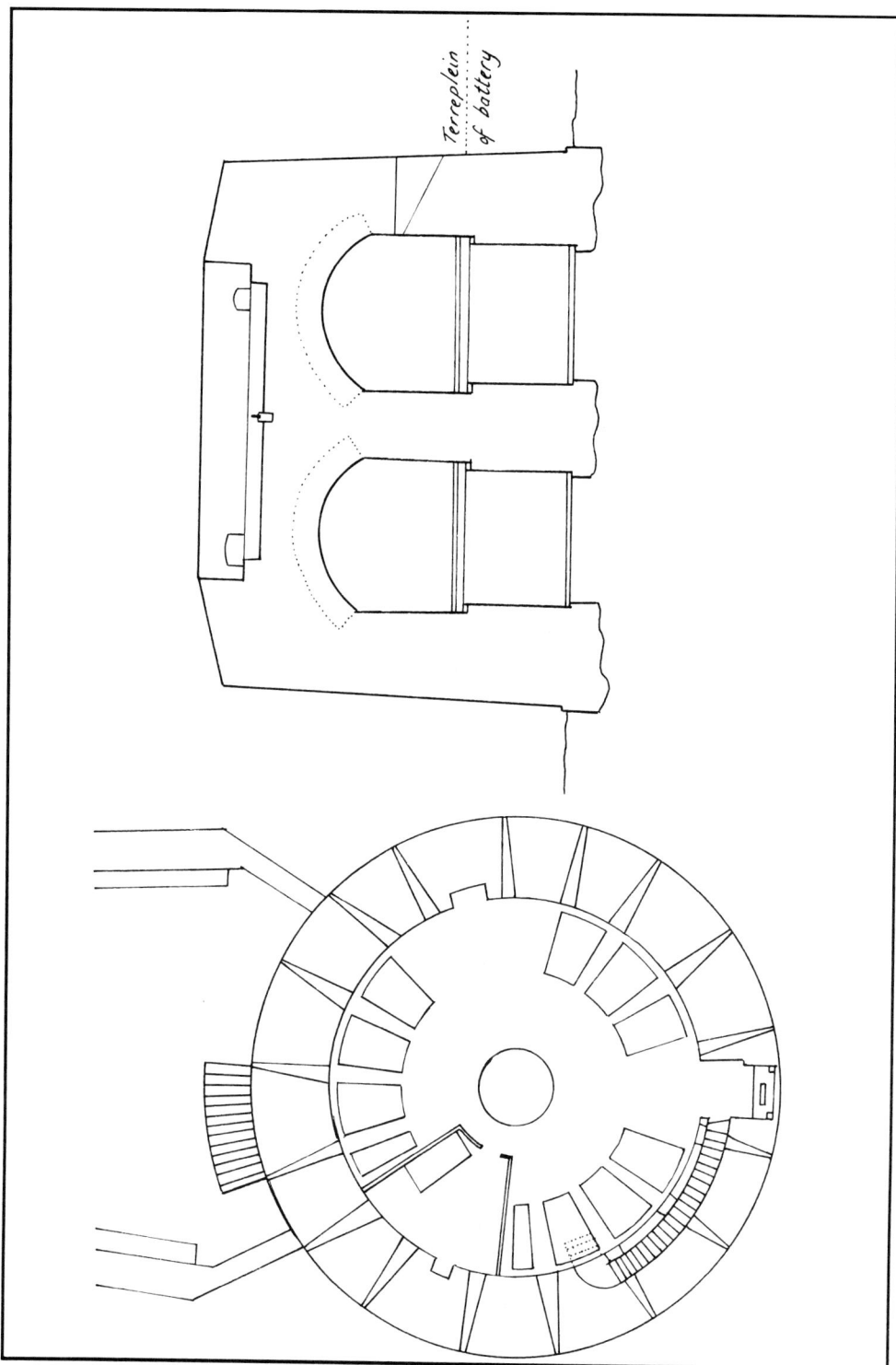

Plan and Section of a Tower
Proposed to be attached to
Fort Pembroke.

*Public Record Office Ref.*
*MPH 868 (m) BC 2740*

Terreplein of battery

# MARTELLO TOWERS PROPOSED BUT NOT BUILT

In 1809 there were proposals to build towers in Alderney. A suggestion was made to build a Sussex Tower (Martello) at Herbe and Hommet (the entrance to Longy Bay)[8]. The idea of building towers was still being considered in Alderney as late as 1849- "A notice to contractors and builders: Martello towers on Hommett, Longy and Rat Island . . . . . . specification from Fort George by 16th January 1849."[9] Although it seems that preparations were well underway the towers were never built and I can only speculate that their non-construction was a result of Government cut backs or a reduced threat of invasion to the islands.

In Guernsey it was suggested that Rocque de Guet, an existing Telegraph establishment, would make an excellent Military post. "The summit of the rock should be levelled . . . . . . and a tower built upon it, capable of mounting four heavy guns upon traversing platforms."[10] This recommendation was not followed through perhaps because the treacherous west coast made a landing highly improbable. Also at Mont Cuet additional protection of Grand Havre was required and it was suggested that "a redoubt or tower construction (be built) upon it."[11] The 1841 report recommended that a tower be connected to Fort Pembroke. A surprising feature here is that the tower was pierced with loop holes as the drawing shows[12]. The last tower that I have found recommended but not constructed was to have strengthened the west coast at Les Vardes.[13]

8. *P.R.O. W.O. 1/605 Report on defence by Brig. Gen. Este 6th February 1809.*

9. *P.R.O. W.O. 55/815 Notice in file.*

10. *P.R.O. W.O. 30/57 Report 1803 Mackelcan*

11. *P.R.O. W.O. 30/57 Report 1803 Mackelcan.*

12. *See Drawing opposite.*

13. *P.R.O. W.O. 55/815.*

# BREHON TOWER

The last tower built in the Channel Islands, was in fact not a Martello tower at all, but an elliptical tower on a rock called "Brehon" halfway between Guernsey and Herm. It was built by Thomas Charles de Putron, from Herm granite. It was started in 1854 and finished in 1856 at a total cost of £8098 18s. 10d..

Sir George Murray, (Master of Ordnance) stated in January 1844 that in his opinion Martello towers should be maintained for public service only, as they were not a suitable means of defence against invaders.

Brehon Tower, (1856)

# Castle Cornet

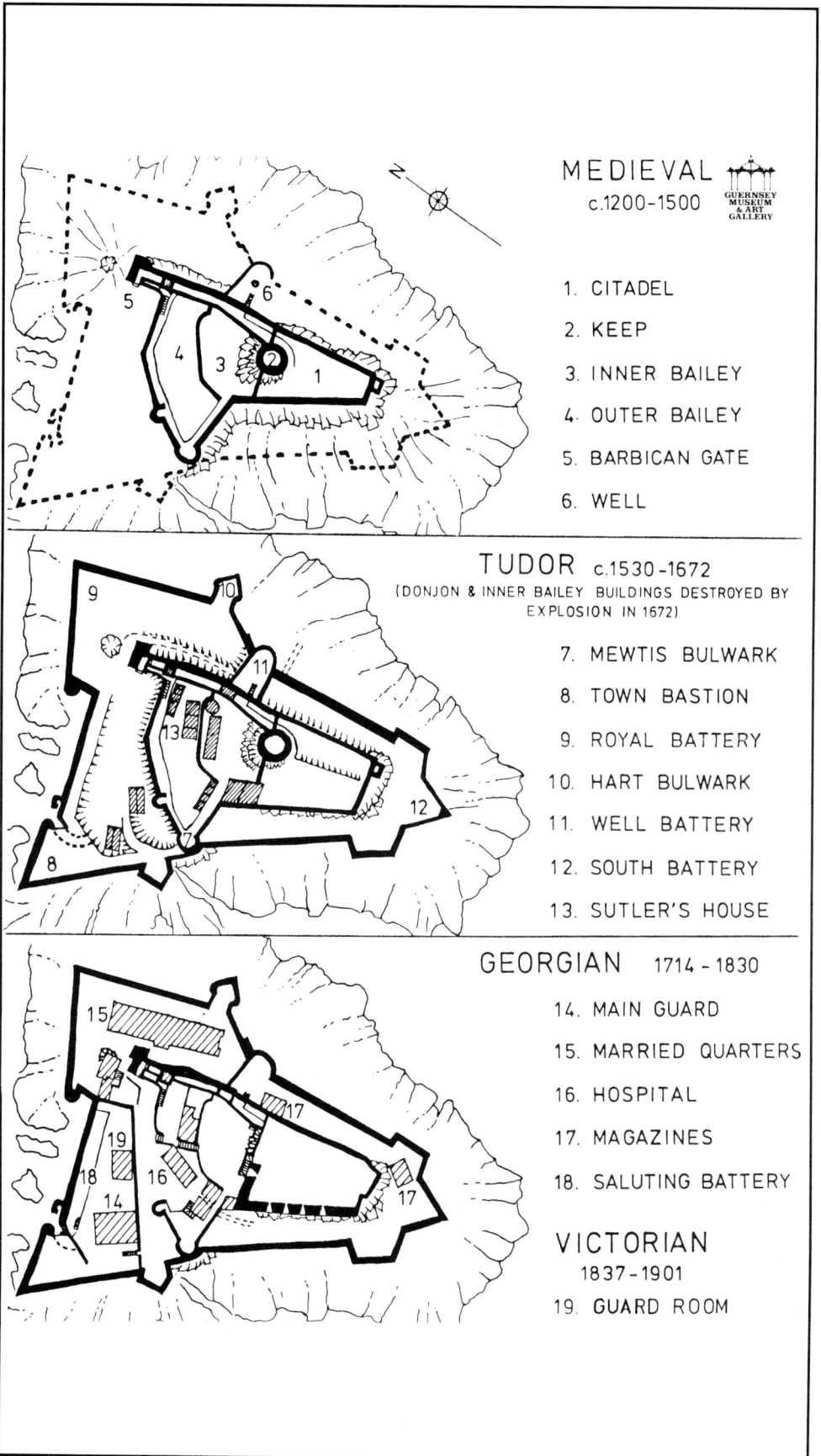

MEDIEVAL
c.1200-1500

GUERNSEY
MUSEUM
& ART
GALLERY

1. CITADEL

2. KEEP

3. INNER BAILEY

4. OUTER BAILEY

5. BARBICAN GATE

6. WELL

TUDOR c.1530-1672
(DONJON & INNER BAILEY BUILDINGS DESTROYED BY
EXPLOSION IN 1672)

7. MEWTIS BULWARK

8. TOWN BASTION

9. ROYAL BATTERY

10. HART BULWARK

11. WELL BATTERY

12. SOUTH BATTERY

13. SUTLER'S HOUSE

GEORGIAN 1714 - 1830

14. MAIN GUARD

15. MARRIED QUARTERS

16. HOSPITAL

17. MAGAZINES

18. SALUTING BATTERY

VICTORIAN
1837-1901

19. GUARD ROOM

The developments of Castle
Cornet from 1200 to the
present day.

# Chapter 6

# Development of Guernsey Forts

*Hougue a la Perre*
*Mont Crevelt*
*Houmet*
*Saumarez*
*Grey*

In this chapter the fortifications will be reviewed in an anti-clock-wise direction excluding the very small 2-3 gun positions, starting in St. Peter Port.

## CASTLE CORNET

A reference must be made to Castle Cornet although it does not have a 'Martello' type tower. It was the principle fort to protect the harbour and town of St. Peter Port. Its history dates from the 13th century to the mid 1800's, but the castle became less important with the improvement of artillery power.

The Museum Education Services diagramatic drawings opposite show the chronological development of the castle. Originally built on an island off the coast it was not until 1860 that the castle was linked to the harbour by a pier and bridge.

Aerial Photograph of Castle Cornet, Guernsey.

## FORT GEORGE

With the continuing unrest between England and France, Fort George was begun in about 1782. The unsuitability of Castle Cornet as the principle fort of the Island, because of its isolated position, was the main reason for the building of a fort that could, if required, withstand a long siege. Fort George also served as the supply base for the garrison and depot for the other island forts.

Fort George commands the hill, south of St. Peter Port, overlooking the town and harbour. Successive Reports (Mackelcan's and Doyle's, 1803) complained that "the works were not complete" but it is generally considered that by 1812 the main fort, lines and batteries were finished. The citadel had a mediaeval appearance with ditches, draw bridges and arrow head ramparts. When finished the fort had eight batteries: Adolphus, Charlotte, Clarence, Kent, Town Point, York, Fausse Braye and Belvedere. The development of Fort George owed much to Sir John Doyle whose name appears over the main gate above the inscription 'G.R.1812'.

During the occupation the Germans built bunkers inside the walls. The fort was outdated for modern warfare but it was an important radar station for the occupying forces. In 1958 the Fort was sold to the States of Guernsey and later sold to private enterprise for open market housing. Now very little remains apart from the perimeter wall Batteries, Belvedere House, Charlotte Battery and the gateway to the fort.

Gateway at Fort George, Guernsey.

# Hougue á la Perre Tower

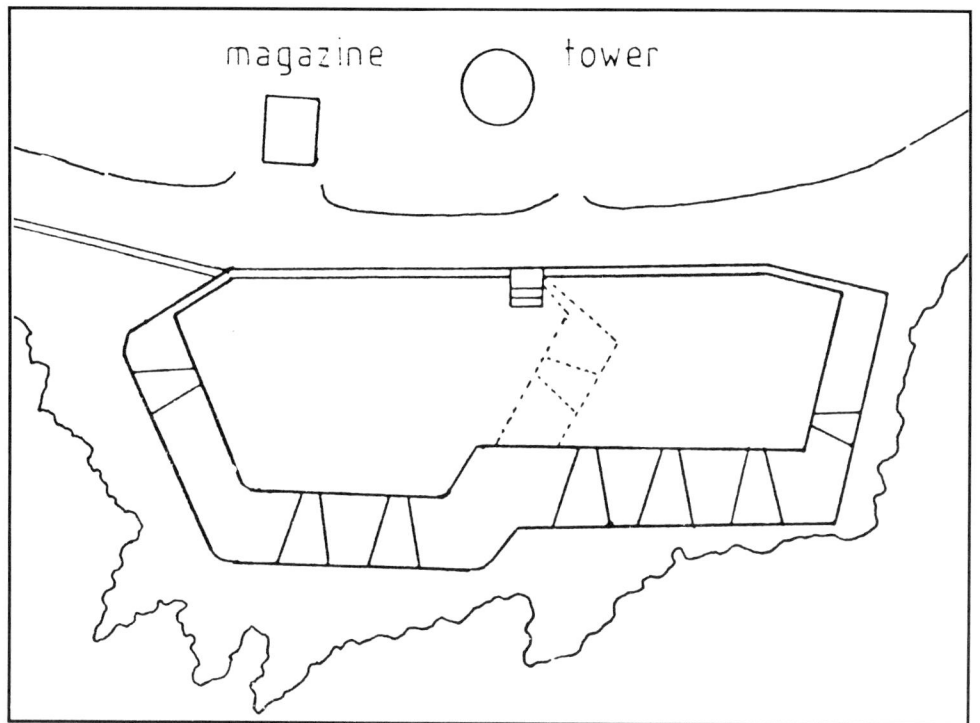

magazine    tower

Hougue á la Perre Fort which was increased in size and numerous reports suggested re-routing the coast road as it divided the fort in two. The Tower was finally demolished in 1905 to make way for road widening and tramsheds.

Hougue á la Perre Tower. Demolished in 1958.

# PRE-MARTELLO TOWERS 1778-1779 (Towers 1-3)

## HOUGUE A LA PERRE (Tower 1)

A battery was known to have been here before 1680 as the Legge Report shows such a fortification. The location was selected to protect the Belle Greve shores. The fort was extended in 1756, and this is recorded in the Actes des Etates, ". . . . . . rebuild with lime and sand and enlarge the Fort of de la Hougue-a-la-Pere".[1] This effectively doubled the size of the fort. (In Chapter 2 a reference is made to the purchasing of the land to build a tower on the hillock adjoining the battery.) The Mackelcan Report[2] proposed to join the battery and tower with a wall in 1803, and re-route the coast road so it would not interfere with the fort. A later report (1842)[3] proposed the same idea. However, the new road was not built, neither was the closing wall across the road.

The wall at the rear of the battery was removed in 1881 when temporary tramway rails were laid and the Les Banques road widened.

The hillock and tower were completely demolished in 1905 to make way for road widening and tramsheds. During the German occupation the fort on the seaward side of the road was extended by the occupying forces. A concrete bunker to cover the approaches to the Belle Greve beach was constructed at the southern end of the fort.

## HOUGUE LA PERE (Tower 2)

A tower was built on this site between 1778-79 to reinforce an existing coastal battery on the shores of Belle Greve beach.

The coastal battery was demolished to widen the road and to enable a new sea wall to be built. In 1958 the tower was removed to build States flats. This was the last of the three towers pulled down and destroyed.

## MONT CREVELT (Tower 3)

The fort at Mont Crevelt is one of the most interesting of the island's military installations. Its history stems over 200 years but unlike many of the island's forts its external appearance remains largely unchanged. In 1680 the Legge Report showed a tower on the crest of Mont Crevelt which was probably only a watch tower. The present tower was built on land purchased by the States in the manner and circumstances already referred to in Chapter 2. The exact date of the tower's construction is not known but it must have been built some time in 1779. It is almost certain that a battery would very early have been built on the north eastern tip of the main island[4] (See page 30) in order to protect the natural harbour of St. Sampson.

1. Actes des Etates 1756 Page 210.

2. P.R.O. W.O. 55/1549 Plan relocated at MPH 161 Report 1803.
3. P.R.O. W.O. 55/1550 Plan relocated at MPH 163 Report 1842.

4. Guernsey was originally two islands separated by a channel called the "Braye du Valle." The channel was slightly west of the Vale Church, Grand Havre, stretching to St. Sampson's bridge. See Pages 39, 40 and 41.

# Mont Crevelt Fort

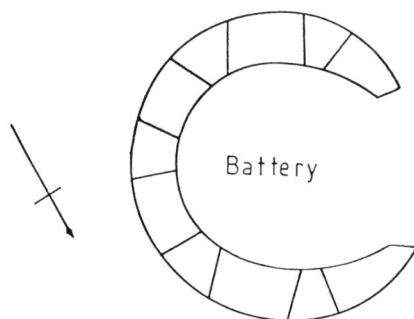

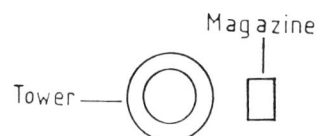

Battery

Tower — Magazine

1803

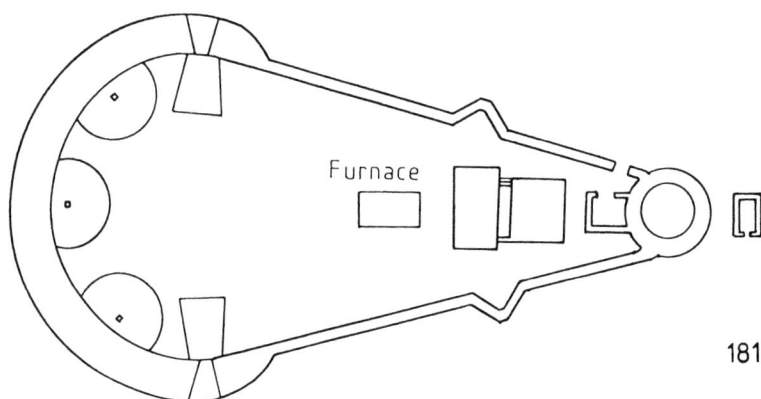

Furnace

1810

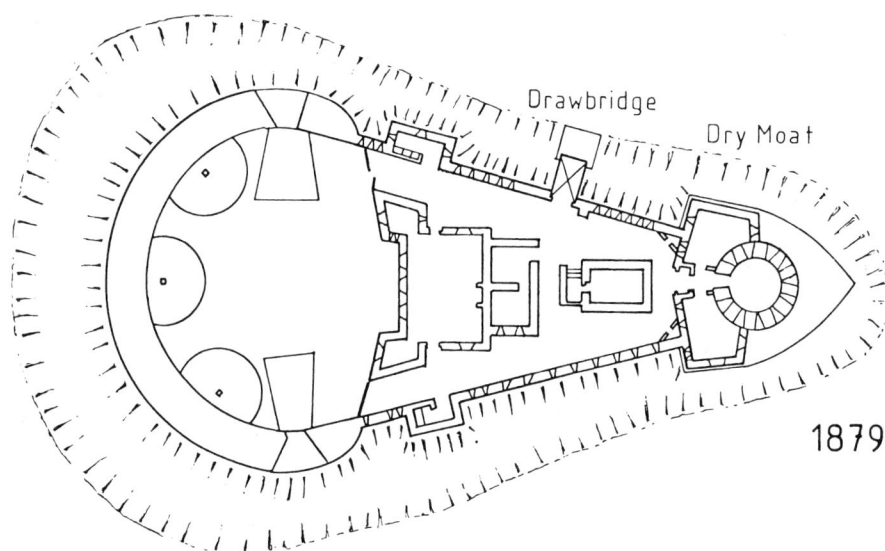

Drawbridge

Dry Moat

1879

Mont Crevelt Fort's exterior appearance has remained virtually unchanged for 200 years.

Mont Crevelt Tower, Guernsey.

A crescent shaped battery "Large enough for 5 guns" was built below the tower in 1805 and paid for by the treasury[5] and this replaced a sod built battery constructed by the States in 1779.[6] The Lieutenant Governor, Sir John Doyle, recommended that "for better protection the battery should be connected to the tower"[7]. This recommendation was completed in 1808 at a cost of £1,600 of which the States were prepared to contribute £750.[8] The walls connecting the battery to the tower were built with a projecting arrow head rampart so the walls could be protected in a siege by giving a cross-fire along the wall. On the west side of the tower a stone lintel shows the original entrance to the building which was blocked up when it became joined to the redoubt. The furnace at this fort became the pattern for later furnaces built in other Island forts.[9] In 1815 repairs were made to the merlons and scarfre and the embrazures filled up, the total cost being £140.

A powder magazine was built near the tower in 1779 but a new powder magazine was built inside the walls was constructed at Doyle's request in 1808.[10] The armament was increased in 1842 when the 5 x 24-pounder guns were replaced by one 64 pounder (monks) and 4 x 32-pounder guns. In 1854 the officers' quarters and the fort were improved by removing the arrowhead rampart and building a rectangular projection. A dry ditch was dug and a drawbridge installed and evidence of these amendments to the fortification can still be seen on the inside of the present entrance. In the 1870's the fortification became obsolete and was bought by the States from the Crown in 1899. Also in that year the tower was transformed into a metal seawater storage tank holder which was bolted together inside the tower necessitating the removal of the floor. A gas engine pumped seawater into the tank which was then used to wash down the quays.[11]

The main building was used as an isolation hospital ward for cholera victims in 1900. Each year money was allocated for this purpose, as these appear in the Billet d'Etats reports,[12] but I believe the money so allocated was never used.

The fort was used by the German occupying forces during World War II. A bunker was constructed inside the battery (which is not visible from outside) and a tunnel connected it with the outside trenches. A machine gun platform was also built on the roof of the living quarters. (The fort is now used by the Northern Venture Scout Unit).

## PRE MARTELLO TOWERS 1778 - 1779 (Towers 4-15)

Tower 4 can be found near Fort L'Angle where Fort Le Marchant now stands. (Fort L'Angle at L'Ancresse is not to be confused with the German Observation Tower near Pleinmont also called Fort L'Angle). This area of L'Ancresse has the most likely landing beaches for an enemy, so it is not surprising that this area had seven towers built in it between 1778-1779.

5. Greffe: Lieutenant Governor's Letter book: Built by Thomas Henry at a cost of £300.
6. P.R.O. W.O. 44/73 1815 Report referring to battery.
7. P.R.O. W.O. 55/1549 1803 Report by General Doyle.
8. P.R.O. W.O. 55/808 Letter 3rd August, 1810.

9. Greffe: Lieutenant Governor Letter book: 1803-1806.

10. Mossprint: shows clearly the side elevation and entrance.

11. At this time the harbour was used for the exportation of granite and importation of coal.
12. Billet d'Etats May 17th 1899.

L'Ancresse Tower No. 6, Guernsey.

59

# Gun Batteries

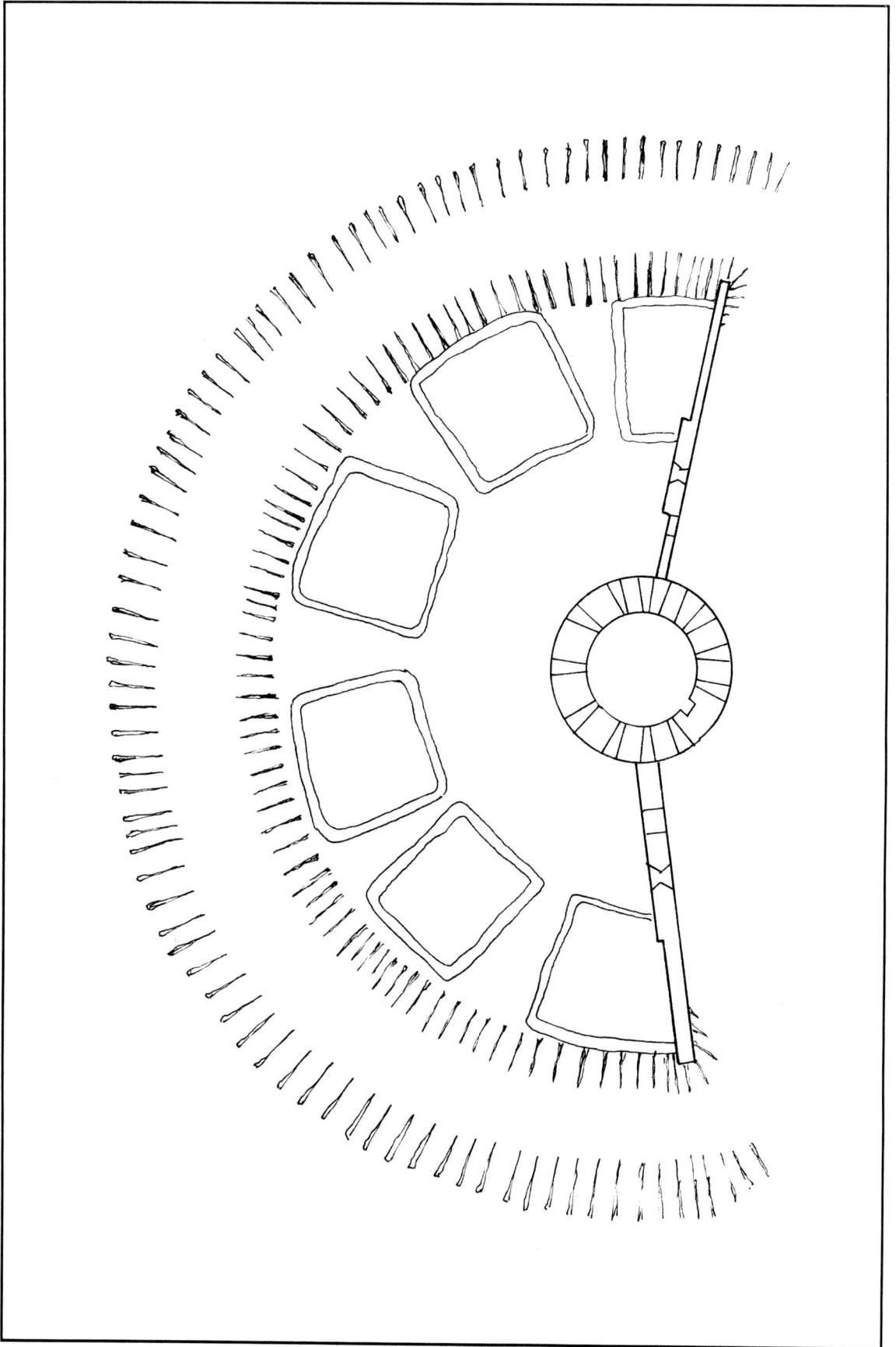

Sketch of
Rousse Battery,
Guernsey.
*Public Records Office
WO 55/1550*

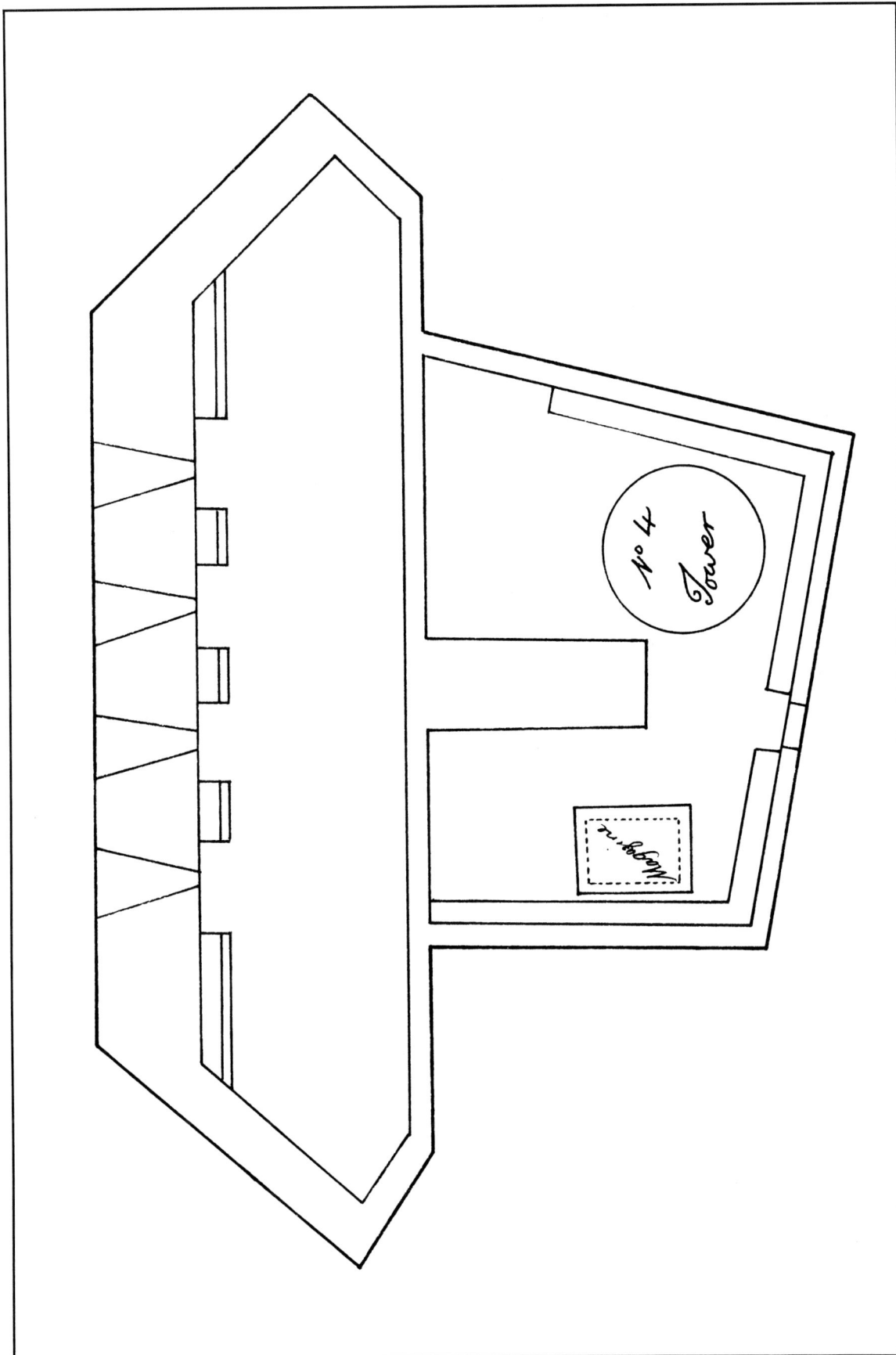

Gun
Batteries

Sketch of Vazon
Battery, Guernsey.
*Ownership of Forts
Report Commissioned by
the Bailiff, 1848.
By Permission of the
Guernsey Greffe.*

# Houmet
# Point

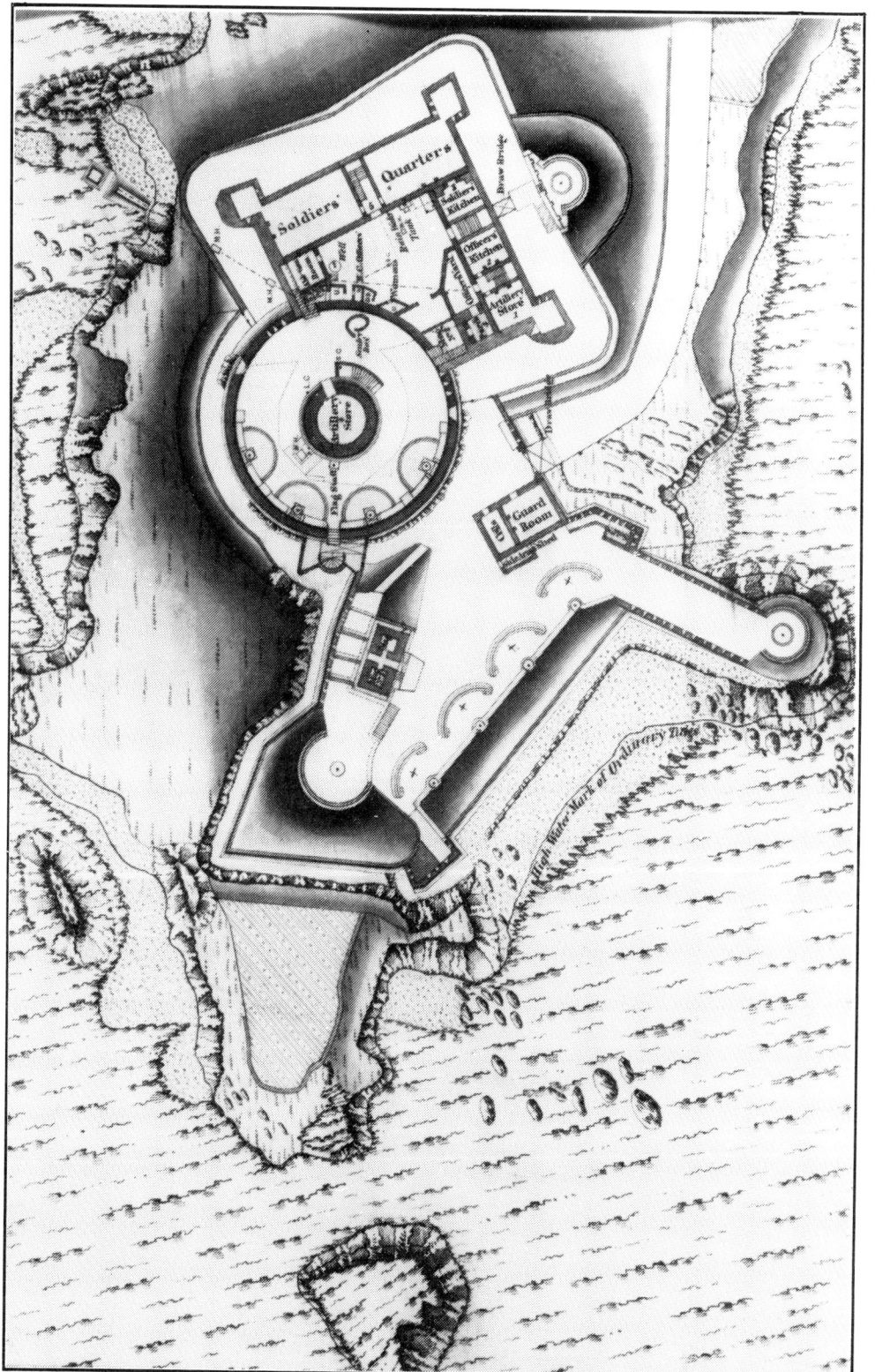

Rousse Tower, Guernsey.

Towers 5, 6, 7, 8 and 9 form a horseshoe around L'Ancresse and Pembroke bays supporting several coastal batteries. In 1842 a report recommended connecting the L'Ancresse right battery to the tower as at Mont Crevelt. Tower number 8, situated near the Golf Club House, was demolished during the German occupation as it interfered with the field of fire of one of their gun batteries. It was the second tower to be demolished. The towers were built close enough together (500 yards apart) so that any attacking force would be caught in a cross-fire.

Tower 10 is at Chouet headland and Tower 11 at Rousse. These stand opposite each other at Grand Havre which is a natural harbour and outlet of the Braye du Valle. The tower at Rousse had a semi-circular earth bulwark with a wall built out from the tower. This was a later development but no date can safely be given to when it was actually built.

The four remaining towers are situated at Vazon, Petit Bôt, Saints Bay and Fermain. Tower 12 at Vazon formed part of the comprehensive defence of the longest beach on the Island. Many Batteries were built along the coastline and reinforced between 1779-1782.

Vazon Tower, Guernsey.

Towers 13, 14, 15 dominate small bays and were supported by batteries on the cliffs and foreshore. It is interesting to note that the powder magazines were built some way away from the towers. This is possibly a result of the experience at Castle Cornet in 1672 when lightning struck the powder magazine and demolished much of the higher levels of the castle including the Keep.

## HOUMET POINT (See plan opposite)

There has been a fort on this headland for a very long time and the Legge Report map[13] shows this clearly. The later survey map[14] shows a number of batteries in the area and a barrack further inland. The Mackelcan Report recommended that "a solid battery should be built here."[15] For some reason, as yet unknown, for it was not originally planned, a tower was built inside the circular wall in 1804. The specifications were: 25' high from foundation, 20' diameter and the wall thickness 5.5' at the bottom reducing to 4.5' at the top. A significant amount of money was spent by the States in 1803 when the existing fort was extended and linked with the outer defences by a caponier. A barrack block for the garrison was built on the landward side of the solid battery wall two storeys high. During the occupation the Germans built a number of bunkers in the area -some on the existing batteries. A hole was made in the outer wall and another into the side of the Martello tower to facilitate the moving of searchlights into position. The site was bought from the Government in 1958 and the Royal Engineers demolished the barracks adjoining the fort the same year.

13. Legge Report 1680.
14. Richmond map 1787.

15. P.R.O. W.O. 55/1549 Report 1803 29th August, 1803.

# Fort
# Saumarez

Fort Saumarez, Guernsey as
it was and as it is now with
it's German bunkers built
underneath.

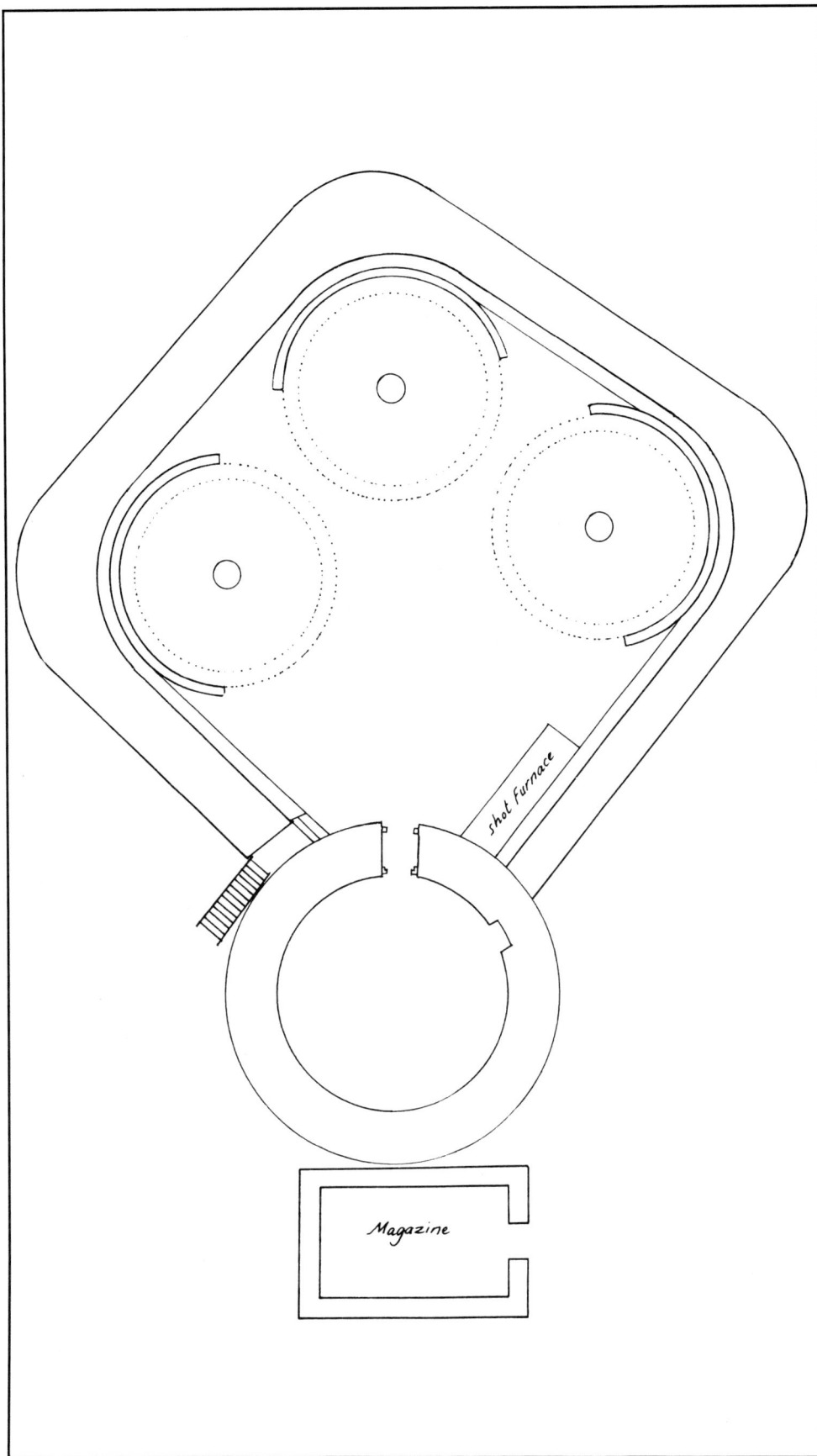

Shot Furnace

Magazine

Plan of fort.
*Public Records Office MPH 868*

# Fort Grey

Château
de Rocquaine

1680

Rocquaine Castle

1803

Fort Grey

1810

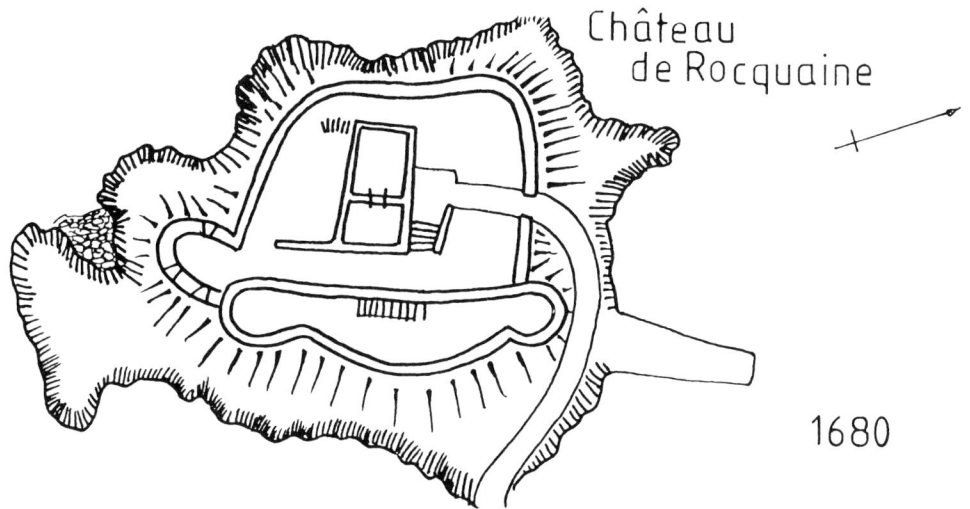

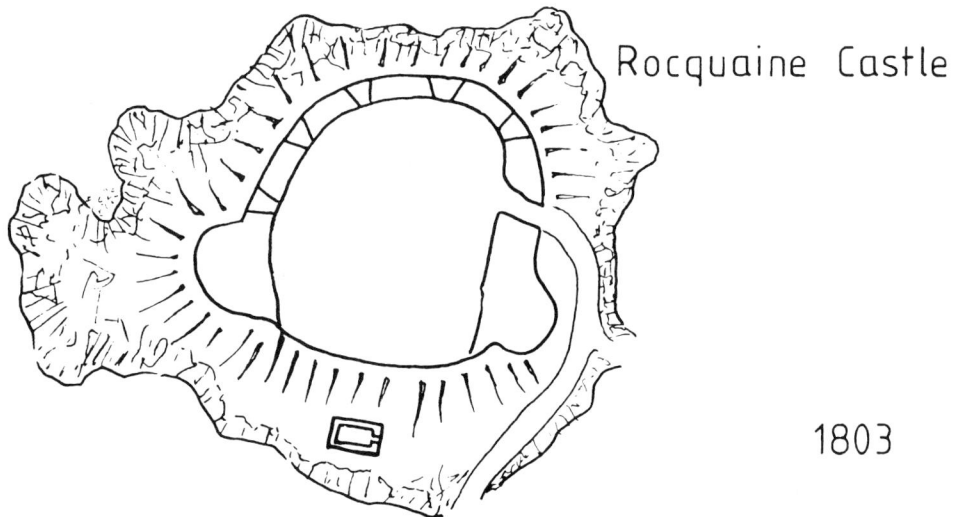

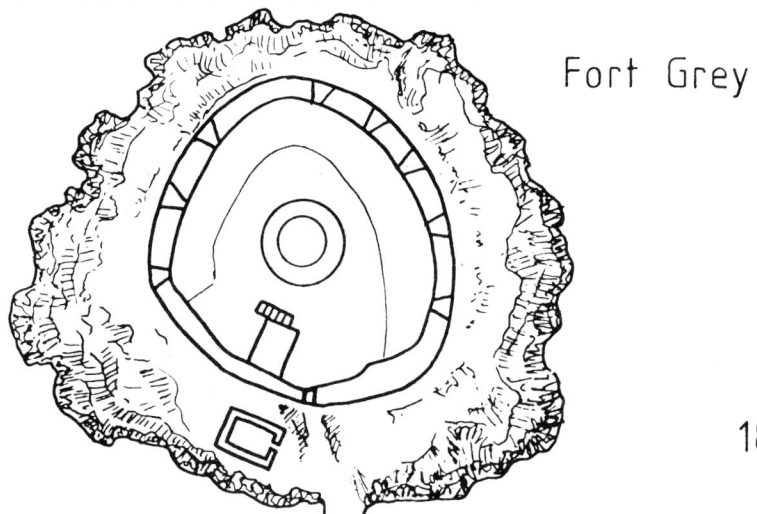

Fort Grey
or
Rocquaine
Castle,
Guernsey.

# FORT SAUMAREZ (See plans on pages 38 and 64)

The headland at Fort Saumarez overlooks the island of Lihou, L'Eree Bay and Perelle Bay and consequently numerous batteries have been built along its coastline. The heights of the headland were used for the telegraph. Flags by day and lanterns by night were used to transfer the messages along the west coast. General Doyle stated in his report (1803) "The original project drawn up by the Commanding Royal Engineer, (Mackelcan) for the construction of a work on the summit of this Commanding Height, was to Enlarge the present Battery, and place three Traversing platforms in it, and to build a tower in its Gorge. . . The Enlargement of the Battery, and the Traversing Platforms are already executed, . . . . . . but the States will not consent to build a Tower."[16] This possibly accounts for the battery being adjoined to the Tower unlike Fort Grey and Houmet. This particular work was completed in 1804 and later other buildings were sited near the tower, the powder magazine being built outside the tower and battery. During the occupation the rock was tunnelled by the Germans and many bunkers built and gun and searchlight positions established around the headland. The roof of the tower was removed and a concrete watch tower was built on top. The inside of the tower was reinforced and linked to the underground tunnel.

16. P.R.O. W.O. 55/1549 General Doyle's Report 1803.

## FORT GREY or ROCQUAINE CASTLE

This fort was built on a small promontory in the bay and could be reached by a causeway at low tide. This was the site of Chateau de Rocquaine. Its early history is unknown. In 1680 it appears in the survey by Colonel Legge. He records that "the battlements want some small repair to a new doore which will make it very strong".[17] In 1803 the Commanding Officer of the Royal Engineers recommended the destruction of the old chateau, when he said " . . . . . . the only project therefore for reform and improvement to be recommended is that of demolishing the present ruins, and building a proper revetment to the battery so as to render it unassailable.

There appears to be a space sufficient in the rear of the battery for a small barrack or tower . . . . . . . "[18] The recommendation of rebuilding a semi-circular redoubt was undertaken by the States, for General Doyle, Lieutenant Governor, reported "The old Castle has been pulled down, the summit of the Rock levelled, and a very powerful Battery erected, capable of containing 12-14 guns. The Battery is of a semi-circular form, projected in front by a solid wall 220 feet in length, from 16-18 feet in height, and from 6-10 feet in thickness. There is also a continued range of platform of 220 feet in length, and 18 feet in breadth, paved with solid granite. But this work still remains to be closed in the rear, and to have a casement or Bombproof lodgement built upon it, for the accommodation of the Garrison."[19]    The powder

17. Bailiff's Library: Colonel Legge Report 1680.

18. P.R.O. W.O. 30/57 Mackelcan Report 1803 Page 314.

19. P.R.O. W.O. 55/1549 General Doyle's Report 1803.

# Guernsey Forts

Fort Houmet, Guernsey 1958, showing demolished barracks. Photograph also shows a German bunker built within the walls of the original fort.

Fort Saumarez, Guernsey, showing German Occupation Tower (1942) built on top of existing Martello Tower.

magazine was again built outside the walls and in 1809, at Doyle's insistence, another one was built inside the fort.[20]

In 1804 a tower was built in the centre of the redoubt and as a result of its new appearance the whole fortification has become affectionately known locally as the "Cup and Saucer". Fortunately, the Germans did not do too much structural damage. They removed several gun ports and pierced the southern side of the lower part of the tower, but did little else.

20. *Actes des Etats 1809 Page 230.*

Fort Grey or Rocquaine Castle, situated on the west coast of Guernsey.

# Map

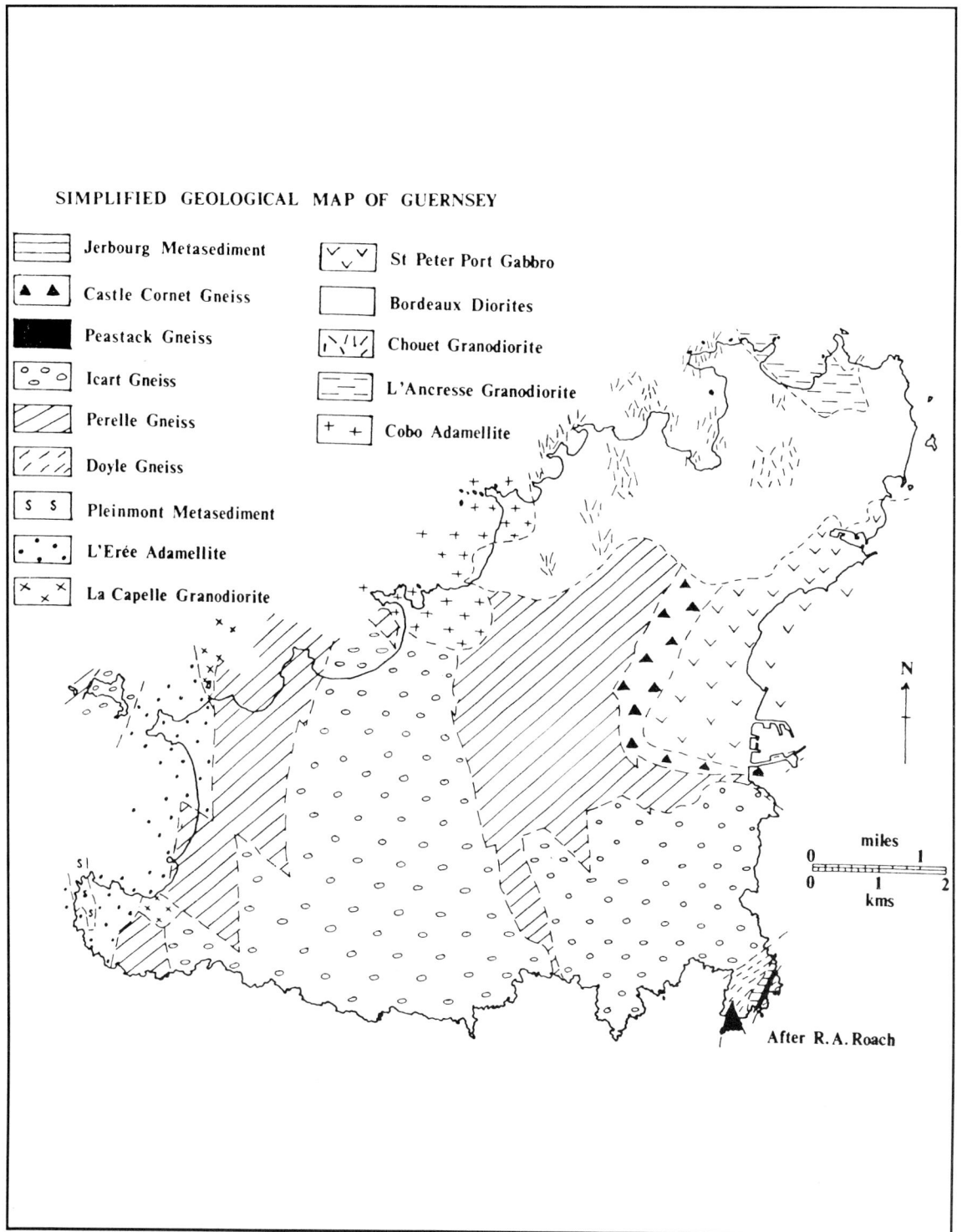

SIMPLIFIED GEOLOGICAL MAP OF GUERNSEY

| | | | |
|---|---|---|---|
| Jerbourg Metasediment | | St Peter Port Gabbro |
| Castle Cornet Gneiss | | Bordeaux Diorites |
| Peastack Gneiss | | Chouet Granodiorite |
| Icart Gneiss | | L'Ancresse Granodiorite |
| Perelle Gneiss | | Cobo Adamellite |
| Doyle Gneiss | | |
| Pleinmont Metasediment | | |
| L'Erée Adamellite | | |
| La Capelle Granodiorite | | |

N

miles
0 1
0 1 2
kms

After R. A. Roach

Simplified
Geological
Map of
Guernsey.

*Chapter 7*

# Building Materials

It is not unusual for builders to use the nearest materials to hand; so it is not surprising that when the earth sod batteries were rebuilt it was with granite. Often in the "Acts des Etats" the phrase "in sand and lime" was used, and naturally granite was the building stone. Guernsey, for such a small island (7 x 4 miles at its widest points), is indeed fortunate to have such a choice of coloured granites. When building the fortifications the nearest quarry supplied the stone, so the towers built at Houmet and Vazon were built from a pink granite (Cobo adamellite) quarried in the area.[1]

*1. See Geological map opposite.*

From the Nicholas de Garis journal,[2] it can be seen that some of the stone for the Petit Bôt tower was prepared at the Petit Bôt site. The journal makes reference to a blue stone specifically as though it was the face stone. Reading through the inventory of materials it is quite staggering to note the number of cart trips that were made to facilitate the building of the tower. At one time there were over 200 quarries in Guernsey-most of them being worked in the north of the island where the bulk of the fortifications were. Obviously transportation was difficult, and there are numerous references to the poor state of the roads.

*2. Journal of Nicholas de Garis - page 22, Translation page 23.*

There are fourteen types of stone to be found in the island and geologically they are not strictly in the granite family (The stone industry at one time was very important to the Guernsey economy.[3]). The stone was exported to England and peak production was reached before the First World War. The last sizeable export was in 1967.

*3. Taken from Societe Guernesiaise Vol. XXI part II page 208.*

## BRICKS

There have been a number of references to bricks being used in the building of the towers and fortifications. These were all produced in the island and at one time there were 22 kilns producing pots and bricks. Brick production takes place in the open, and therefore it is dependant upon the weather. The two kilns still standing at Oatlands are typical of the kilns used for the production of bricks in the island and the photographs of Best Brickfield (Page 72) give some idea of the space required to stack the bricks at various stages of production.[4]

*4. This photograph was taken at the turn of the century. 1900.*

# Brickfield

Best Brickfield 1901.

*by permission*
*Mr. E. B. Best*

# Chapter 8

# Guernsey Militia Armament of Forts and Towers

Colour Sergeant of the Grenadiers and Rifleman, 1833.

## THE GUERNSEY MILITIA

The formation of the Guernsey Militia grew out of the Norman feudal system as already mentioned in the introduction. Its purpose was to support the garrison and to man the batteries and forts around the coast in times of war. Alarm posts were established as assembly points when the alarm guns were sounded. "In 1750 the Militia comprised 1,800 soldiers commanded by three colonels, twenty captains, three majors, fifteen lieutenants, sixteen ensigns and the additional fifty-eight sergeants and fifteen drummers, by the end of the century officers and men totalled 2,729."[1]

The Guernsey regiments were formed by regions: North, South, East (Town). The West Regiment and the Guernsey Militia Artillery were formed in 1780 by Colonel Nicholas Dobree thus being added to the other three Regiments. These regiments could be recognized by their different colour facings. In order to decieve the enemy the Royal Court ordered that all who could afford a uniform of red coats and white stockings should buy them out of their own savings whilst those less fortunate could seek parish assistance. It was not until 1782 that the government paid for such uniforms after being lobbied by the States. A corps of cavalry was formed in 1796; the men being paid 2s. 6d. daily for man and horse.

Great emphasis was laid on gunnery skills and techniques but it was not until 1801 that red clothes were issued to the heavy gunners. The militia had to report each Sunday for drill and practice. Boys of fourteen and over not attached to any corps were obliged to attend Sunday parades and exercises. The sons of Methodists professing the religion of their parents had to assemble for exercise every Monday.

## ARMAMENT

The 1680 Legge Survey lists the guns mounted in Guernsey, together with recommendations for further armaments, as follows:-

*Plaiderie (possibly Le Tour Grand): 2 x iron sakers.*
*West End of Town 1 iron saker.*
*Hougue a la Perre, Bulwark: 1 x demy culverin, 1 x minion (in need of a carriage) iron.*
*North of above: 1 x 6-pounder; 1 x iron saker. Two extra demy culverins were recommended: At the Key de la Viatte faceing to St.Sans (St. Sampson), an iron demy culverin.*
*At the bulwark Cotamanse, faceing Arme (Herm) and Jerau (Jethou): 1 x demy culverin; 1 x falcon, iron; 2 x 12-pounders were needed as well.*

1. *"Royal Guernsey" A history of the Royal Guernsey Militia.*

# Gun
# Drill

Gun drill on SBML coast
guns.

*Photographs - "The Royal Artillery
Institution, Woolwich."*

*Belgrave Fort: 1 x demy culverin; 1 x falcon, iron. 2 x 12-pounders also needed.*
*Vale Castle: 1 x minion; 1 x falcon, iron; 3 x demy culverins needed as well.*
*Mont Crevet Mount: 2 x iron sakers. 4 x 12-pounders needed as well.*
*Fort de l'Angle: East of Lancras: (On site of Ft. le Marchant): 3 x 12-pounder needed on ship carriages. It covered vessels approaching the harbour.*
*Nicq de Herbe Lancras: 1 x iron 8-pounder. Another one was recommended.*
*La Corbiere de Lancras: a musquett shot west of Nicq: 1 x iron saker. 2 additional 12-pounder were wanted.*
*Middle of Lancras: 1 x iron saker. Instead there should be 2 x demy culverins.*
*Near above: 1 x demy culverins.*
*Near above: 1 x iron saker. Another 12-pounder was wanted.*
*Houmet Nicol (on which stands Fort Houmet): 1 x saker. 4 x 12-pounders needed as well.*
*Vazon: 3 x iron sakers. 2 x 12-pounders needed as well.*
*West of Vazon: An iron saker. To this should be added 2 x demy culverin.*
*Rocquaine Castle: An iron saker. This should be augmented by 3 x 12-pounders.The fishermen said that many vessels sheltered there in fowle weather."*[2]

2. *Bailiff's Library "Col. Legge Survey 1680".*

When the French joined the Americans as allies in 1778 there was a shortage of ordnance in the Channel Islands. The Governors of both islands requested artillery to protect the islands from invasion. General Conway, Governor of Jersey, received a letter from the Board of Ordnance:- "I much fear we have few or no cannon to spare at present from the opinion of the Board . . . . . I have desired the Board to procure as much good Iron Ordnance as possible for those defensive services, so much called for . . . . . The Amusettes and long three's mounted on travelling carriages are very useful in many parts of war and I have been a strong advocate for them." Signed Townsend.[3] Townsend also added that there were no Officers available for instructing in artillery at that time.

3. *P.R.O. W.O. 46/11 Letter from Board of Ordnance to General Conway.*

By 1800 the ordnance in the island had increased, and the earlier names of demi-culverin, saker, curtal and cannon-perier had fallen out of use and the guns were now referred to as 6-, 12-, 18-, 24- and 32-pounders. The 1801 Report shows the armament in the island at that time.[4] (Pages 79 and 80).

4. *P.R.O. W.O. 55/808 Report on Batteries Col. Mackelcan 1st August 1801.*

General Doyle was appointed Lieutenant Governor in 1803. He brought with him a great deal of military experience and quickly prepared the island for defence. In his report he recommended mounting carronades on top of the 15 towers.[5] Mounting 12 pounder

5. *P.R.O. W.O. 55/1549 Doyle Report on the defence of Guernsey 1803.*

# Traversing
# Frame

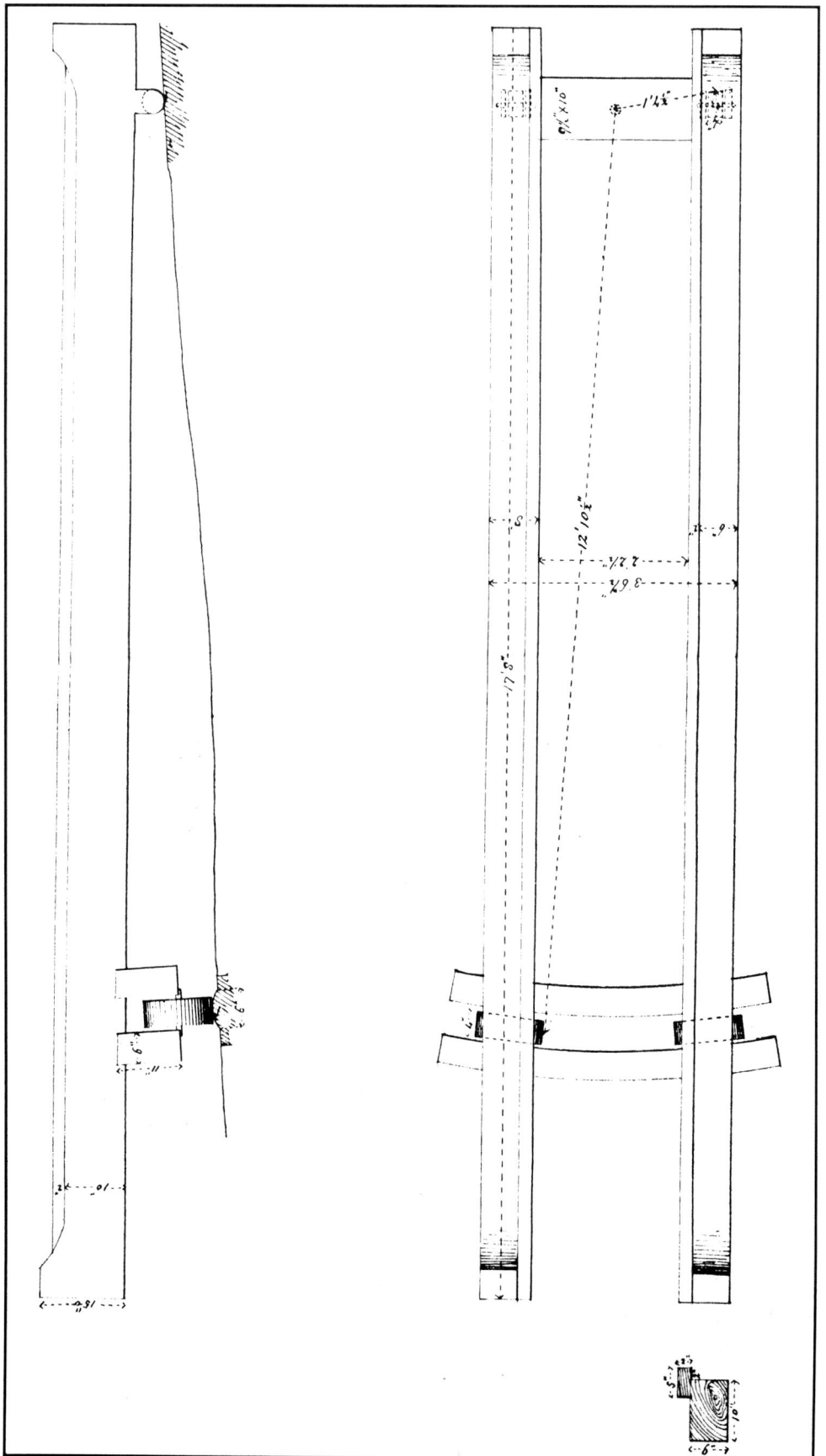

Plan of Traversing Frame for
gun used in Guernsey.

*Public Records Office*
*Ref. WO 44/78*

76

on top of the early towers was only made possible with the invention of the carronade. Carronades first came into use in 1779 and were made by the Carron Company (Scottish Ironfounders). They were lighter and shorter in length with a larger calibre than ordinary ordnance. They were an immediate success with the Royal Navy, where they were nicknamed "smashers", as they suited their tactics for close combat. The carronades were mounted on sliding wooden carriages which could be traversed. I believe that, because of their comparative short range of only 450 yards, their use on the towers was to fire grapeshot[6] to injure any soldiers attempting to attack or besiege the tower. When the three Martello towers were built on the west coast they were mounted with 24-pounder carronades.

The plan, elevation and section (page 78) show an 18-pounder gun on Colonel Congreve's principle with trucks on the trunnions and mounted on a traversing platform adapted for the top of a tower in Jersey in 1813. Colonel Humfrey (R.E.) claims that the 18-pounder was manned by three men and fired 8 rounds in 12 minutes 55 seconds compared with the old pattern manned by five men and which fired 8 rounds in 15 minutes 32 seconds.

Traversing platforms were introduced into the island forts bringing greater efficiency (i.e. a better rate of rapid fire and less men required to position the gun ) see the photographs (page 74). Traces of the semi-circular tracks can still be seen in some of the island forts. With the defeat of Napoleon at Waterloo in 1815, and the immediate threat of attack from France withdrawn, the 1817 report[7] recommended dismantling a number of the guns in the island. (Page 81-84).

*6. Grape shot "a combination of balls" weighing each 2 lb (12 for a 24 pr.) which were packed into a cylindrical canvas bag of the size of the cannon ball generally used in the gun.*

*7. P.R.O. W.O. 44/540 Report Col. De Butts 3rd September 1817.*

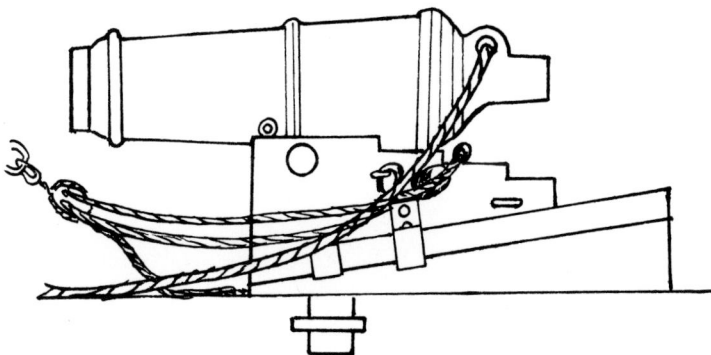

"The Smasher".
Carronade mounted on inclined carriage slide as equipped in the British Navy of the time.

# Gun Platform on Jersey Tower

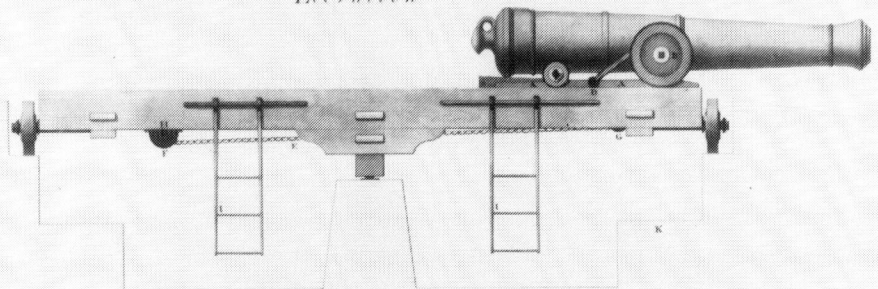

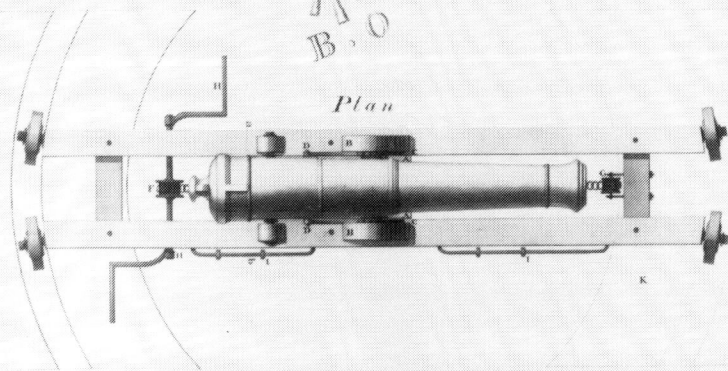

Plan Elevation and Section of an 18 pr. gun mounted on traversing platform.

Report of the Coast Batteries in the Island of Guernsey, specifying their situations, and the Ordnance mounted upon them. — ~~...~~ 1st August 1801.

| Names of Batteries | Situation | Ordnance Mounted No. | Natures Pr |
|---|---|---|---|
| South Pier | At St Peter's Town | 1 | 6 |
| North Do | Ditto | 2 | 24 Carr.d |
| Amherst | North end of St Peter's Town | 7 | 20 |
| Sellery | Ditto | 3 | 24 |
| Arrivée | North East of Do upon a rising ground 400 Yards from the Shore | 3 | 18 |
| Pervin | Near the long Store | 8 | 23 |
| Hougue a'la parez | Center of Belle greve Bay | 8 | 24 |
| Belle greve | North of Hougue a'la parez | 4 | 20 |
|  |  | 1 | 9 |
| De Lancey | At De Lancey Barracks | 2 | 23 |
| Mont Creveé | South Pt of Abrahampson's Harbour | 3 | 24 |
| Homet Benit | North of Vale Castle | 1 | 24 |
| Point Noirmont | North of Homet Benit | 1 | 24 |
| Bossuet | North of Noirmont | 2 | 18 |
| L'Angle | East of L'Ancresse Bay | 5 | 24 |
|  | East Side | 1 | 18 |
|  |  | 1 | 12 |
| Batteries in L'Ancresse Bay | Center | 3 | 18 |
|  |  | 2 | 18 |
|  | West Side | 1 | 12 |
|  |  | 1 | 23 |
|  | West Point | 1 | 18 |
| Mont Cuet | North part of Grande Havre | 2 | 24 |
|  |  | 1 | 18 |

Lt Genl Morse Act. Ch. Roy.Ing."

# Report of the Coastal Batteries 1801, Guernsey, *Continued*

| Names of Batteries | Situation | Ordnance Mounted | |
|---|---|---|---|
| | | N° | Nature |
| Rousse | South East of Grand Havre | 2 | 18 |
| Portenlere | South West of Rousse | 1 | 20 |
| Saliries | South West of Portinfer | 1 | 20 |
| Cobo | North East of Hommette | 2 | 20 |
| Rock de Guet | North East of Hommett | 1 | 23 |
| Two Gun Battery | East of Albec | 2 | 23 |
| Batteries at Houmette | North Point of Vason Bay | 4 | 24 |
| | | 2 | 18 Carr |
| Anstauther | On the Heights South of Vason Bay | 2 | 18 |
| Batteries in Vazon Bay | At the Tower | 4 | 23 |
| | At new Storehouse | 4 | 6 |
| | South West of Ditto | 3 | 6 |
| | South West Pt of Vason Bay | 2 | 23 |
| At Le Croque Point | Between Vason & Perelle Bays | 2 | 18 |
| Richmond | North East Pt of Perelle Bay | 1 | 18 |
| | | 2 | 9 |
| Perelle | Perelle Bay | 1 | 0 |
| Druids Altar | South West Pt of Perelle Bay | 2 | 23 |
| Leree | North Pt of Rocquaine Bay | 2 | 18 |
| Rocquaine Castle | In Rocquaine Bay | 2 | 24 |
| | | 2 | 6 |
| Porret | South Point of Ditto | 2 | 18 |
| | | 1 | 9 |
| Batteries in Tibo Bay | West of Icart | 1 | 24 |
| | | 1 | 9 |
| | | 1 | 24 Gun |
| One Gun | Between Tibo & Icart | 1 | 24 |
| Icart | E° between Tibo & Saints Bay | 2 | 24 |
| Saints Bay | North East of Icart | 1 | 24 |
| | | 1 | 9 |
| Moulin Cuet | West of Jerbourg | 2 | 24 |

Report of Coastal Batteries in the Island of Guernsey specifying the Ordnance in them.

*Public Records Office*
*Ref. WO 55/808*

80

# Gun Inspection Report 1816

**Report** *of the Monthly Inspection of the Guns, Ammunition and Stores, at the different Batteries, Magazines, &c. Round the Coast of the Island of Guernsey, between the 1st and 31st October 1816.*

*Per Board's Order, 6th March, 1809.*

| Names of Places where Batteries, &c. are situated. | Description of Batteries, Magazines, &c. | | Total Number of Guns at each place | Dates when the Ammunition was last Aired. | REMARKS. |
|---|---|---|---|---|---|
| | | | | *1816* | |
| FERMAIN | Watch-House | Battery ...... 24 Pr. Gun ...... 1 | | 24 June | |
| | | Permanent Magazine. . . . . . . | | | |
| | Becquet Point | Battery ...... 24 Pr. Gun ...... 1 | | " | |
| | | Portable Magazine. . . . . . . | | | |
| | Left Heights | Battery ...... 6 Pr. Gun ...... 1 | 10 | | |
| | Bottom of the Bay | Battery { 24 Pr. Guns ...... 3 / 24 Pr. Carronade .. 1 | | | |
| | | Tower ...... 12 Pr. Carronade .. 1 | | | |
| | | Permanent Magazine. . . . . . . | | " | The Ammunition & Stores at the different Batteries & Magazines in good Condition |
| | Right of the Bay | Battery ...... 24 Pr. Carronades .. 2 | | | |
| Bedouné | | Battery .. Guns { 12 Pr. ........ 1 / 6 Pr. ........ 2 | 3 | 27 " | |
| | | Permanent Magazine. . . | | | |
| Jerbourg | | Battery ...... 24 Pr. Guns ...... 2 | 2 | 14 Sept | |
| | | Permanent Magazine. . . . . | | | |
| St. Martin's Point | | Battery ...... 24 Pr. Gun ...... 1 | 1 | " | |
| | | Traversing Platform constructed to contain Ammunition | | | |
| Moullin le Huette | | Battery ...... 24 Pr. Guns ...... 2 | 2 | " | |
| | | Permanent Magazine. . . . | | | |
| Heights Right of ditto | | Battery ...... 24 Pr. Gun ...... 1 | 1 | 12 Sept | |
| | | Portable Magazine. . . . . | | | |
| SAINTS BAY | Bottom of the Bay | Battery ...... 18 Pr. Gun ...... 1 | 1 | " | |
| | | Portable Magazine. . . . . | | | |
| | | Tower ...... 12 Pr. Carronade .. 1 | | | |
| | Right Extremity | Battery ...... 24 Pr. Guns ...... 2 | 3 | " | |
| | | Permanent Magazine . . . | | | |
| cart | | Permanent Magazine. . . . | | 13 " | |

81

Report of the monthly inspection of the guns, 31st October, 1816, Guernsey.

P.R.O. WO 44/73

| Names of Places where Batteries, &c. are situated. | Description of Batteries, Magazines, &c. | | Total Number of Guns at each place. | Dates when the Ammunition was last Aired. | REMARKS. |
|---|---|---|---|---|---|
| Right of Icart | Battery ······ 24 pr. Gun ······ | 1 | 1 | *1816* 11 Sept | |
| | Portable Magazine. | | | | |
| Tibbo Bay | Battery ······ 24 pr. Gun ······ | 1 | 2 | — " | |
| | Tower ······ 12 pr. Carronade ··· | 1 | | | |
| | Portable Magazine. | | | | |
| St Lear | Battery ······ 24 pr. Guns ······ | 2 | 2 | 12' " — | |
| | Permanent Magazine. | | | | |
| Soumilleuse | Battery ······ 9 pr. Gun | | 1 | " | |
| | Permanent Magazine | | | | |
| La Tuille | Battery ······ 18 pr. Guns ······ | 2 | 2 | " | |
| | Permanent Magazine. | | | | |
| Narrow Port | Battery ······ 9 pr. Gun ······ | 1 | 1 | 12 " — | |
| | Portable Magazine | | | | |
| Plein Mont | Battery ······ 18 pr. Gun ······ | 1 | 1 | | |
| | Portable Magazine. | | | | |
| Pessery | Battery ······ 18 pr. Guns ······ | 3 | 3 | 6' July | The Ammunition & Stores at the different Batteries and Magazines in good Cond &c |
| | Permanent Magazine. | | | | |
| Rocquain Castle or Fort Grey | Tower ········ 24 pr. Carronade ···· | 1 | 7 | 16' " — | |
| | Battery ······ 24 pr. Guns ····· | 6 | | | |
| | Permanent Magazines, No. 1 and 2. | | | | |
| Rocquain Bay | Battery ······ 18 pr. Guns ······ | 3 | 3 | 9' " — | |
| | Permanent Magazine. | | | | |
| Le Ree Point | Battery ······ 18 pr. Guns ······ | 2 | 2 | | |
| Fort Saumarez | Tower ········ 24 pr. Carronade ···· | 1 | 4 | 15' " — | |
| | Battery ······ 24 pr. Guns ······ | 3 | | | |
| | Permanent Magazine. | | | | |
| Druids Altar | Battery ······ 20 pr. Guns ······ | 2 | 2 | 1' " " | |
| | Permanent Magazine. | | | | |
| Perelle Bay | Battery ······ 20 pr. Guns ······ | 2 | 2 | 12' Sept | |
| | Permanent Magazine. | | | | |
| Fort Richmond | Battery ······ 20 pr. Guns ······ | 4 | 4 | 7' Sept | |
| | Magazines { Permanent. / Portable. | | | | |
| Le Crocq Point | Battery ······ 20 pr. Guns ······ | 3 | 3 | 12' " — | |
| | Permanent Magazine. | | | | |
| Vazon Bay — Left | Battery ······ 20 pr. Guns ······ | 2 | 15 | " " | |
| | Portable Magazine. | | | | |
| Vazon Bay — Blondel | Battery ······ 20 pr. Guns ······ | 3 | | — " | |
| | Portable Magazine. | | | | |
| Vazon Bay — Centre | Battery ······ 20 pr. Guns ······ | 5 | | 14' " " | |
| | Permanent Magazine. | | | | |
| Vazon Bay — Right | Tower ······ 12 pr. Carronade ······ | 1 | | | |
| | Battery ······ 20 pr. Guns ······ | 4 | | | |
| | Permanent Magazine. | | | 19' " " | |

82

| Names of Places where Batteries, &c. are situated. | Description of Batteries, Magazines, &c. | | Total Number of Guns at each place. | Dates when the Ammunition was last Aired. | REMARKS. |
|---|---|---|---|---|---|
| Houmette Point | Batteries ...... | 24 Pr. Guns ...... 2 | 8 | *1816* | |
| | | 24 Pr. Gun ...... 1 | | *25 Sept* | |
| | Tower ...... 24 Pr. Carronade .. 1 | | | | |
| | Battery ...... 24 Pr. Guns ...... 4 | | | | |
| | Magazines.. | Permanent, No. 1 and 2... | | | |
| | | Portable. . . . . | | | |
| Fort Burton | Battery ...... 20 Pr. Guns ...... 4 | | 4 | *3d* | |
| | Magazines.. | Permanent. | | | |
| | | Portable. . . . | | | |
| Rocq de Guette | Battery ...... 20 Pr. Gun ...... 1 | | 1 | *26* | |
| | Permanent Magazine . . . . | | | | |
| Cobbo Bay | Battery ...... 20 Pr. Guns ...... 2 | | 2 | | |
| | Portable Magazine. | | | | |
| Saline Bay | Battery ...... 20 Pr. Gun ...... 1 | | 1 | | |
| Grand Rocq | Battery ...... 24 Pr. Guns ...... 3 | | 3 | *10* | *The Ammunition* |
| | Permanent Magazine . . . . | | | | *and Stores at the* |
| Portenfer | Battery ...... 20 Pr. Gun ...... 1 | | 1 | " | *different Batteries* |
| | Portable Magazine. . . . . | | | | *& Magazines in* |
| Rouse | Tower ...... 12 Pr. Carronade .. 1 | | 4 | *12* | *good condition* |
| | Battery ...... 24 Pr. Guns ...... 3 | | | | |
| | Permanent Magazine. . . . | | | | |
| Pickerie | Battery ...... 18 Pr. Guns ...... 2 | | 2 | " | |
| | Portable Magazine. . . . | | | | |
| Mount Cuette | Tower ...... 12 pr. Carronade .. 1 | | 6 | " | |
| | Batteries .. | 24 Pr. Guns ........ 3 | | | |
| | | 24 Pr. Guns ........ 2 | | | |
| | Permanent Magazine. . . . . | | | | |
| Platon Rocq | Battery ...... 20 Pr. Gun ...... 1 | | 1 | " | |
| | Portable Magazine. . . . | | | | |
| Lancresse Bay | Tower, No. 9.....12 Pr. Carronade .. 1 | | 19 | *11* | |
| | Battery ...... 9 Pr. Gun ...... 1 | | | | |
| | Portable Magazine. . . . | | | | |
| | Tower, No. 8.....12 Pr. Carronade .. 1 | | | | |
| | Battery ...... 20 Pr. Guns ...... 5 | | | | |
| | Portable Magazine. . . . | | " | | |
| | Tower, No. 7.....12 Pr. Carronade .. 1 | | | | |
| | Battery ...... 20 Pr. Guns ...... 4 | | | | |
| | Permanent Magazine. . . . | | " | | |
| | Tower, No. 6.....12 Pr. Carronade .. 1 | | | | |
| | Tower, No. 5.....12 Pr. Carronade .. 1 | | | | |
| | Battery ...... 24 Pr. Guns ...... 3 | | | | |
| | Permanent Magazine. . . . | | *12* | | |
| | Tower, No. 4.....12 Pr. Carronade .. 1 | | | | |
| Fort Le Marchant | Battery ...... 24 Pr. Guns ...... 6 | | 6 | " | |

# Gun Inspection Report 1816 Continued

| Names of Places where Batteries, &c are situated. | Description of Batteries, Magazines, &c. | | Total Number of Guns at each place | Dates when the Ammunition was last Aired. | REMARKS. |
|---|---|---|---|---|---|
| Fort Doyle | Battery ...... 18 pr. Guns ...... 3 | | 3 | 18[?] 24ˢᵗ Sepᵗ | |
| | Store House. | | | | |
| | Portable Magazine | | | | |
| Bousset Point | Battery ...... 24 pr. Guns ...... 2 | | 2 | 16 " | |
| | Permanent Magazine. | | | | |
| Noir Mont Point | Battery ...... 24 pr. Guns ...... 1 | | 1 | " | |
| | Portable Magazine. | | | | |
| Homet Bené | Battery ...... 24 pr. Gun ...... 1 | | 1 | " — | |
| | Portable Magazine. | | | | |
| Vale Castle | Upper Battery .... 9 pr. Guns ...... 2 | | 3 | 23ᵈ Augᵗ | |
| | Lower Battery ·· 24 pr. Gun ...... 1 | | | | |
| | Permanent Magazine. | | | | |
| Mount Crevet | Tower ........12 pr. Carronades ... 1 | | 6 | 9ᵗ Sepᵗ | |
| | Battery ...... 24 pr. Guns ...... 5 | | | | |
| | Permanent Magazine. | | | | |
| Spur Point | Battery ...... 24 pr. Gun ...... 1 | | 1 | — " | The Ammunition and Stores at the diffᵗ Batteries & Magazines in good Condition |
| | Portable Magazine. | | | | |
| De Lancey Barracks | Battery ...... 18 pr. Guns ...... 2 | | 2 | 14ᵗ — " | |
| | Permanent Magazine. | | | | |
| Kemps | Battery ...... 6 pr. Gun. ...... 1 | | 1 | | |
| Belle Greve | Tower ... 12 pr. Carrᵈ. 1 | | 5 | " — | |
| | Battery ...... 18 pr. Guns ...... 4 | | | | |
| | Permanent Magazine. | | | | |
| Houge à la Perre | Tower ........12 pr. Carronade .... 1 | | 10 | — " — | |
| | Battery ...... { 24 pr. Guns ...... 7 | | | | |
| | { 9 pr. Guns ...... 2 | | | | |
| | Permanent Magazine. | | | | |
| Fort Perwin | Battery ...... 20 pr. Guns ...... 4 | | 4 | 12 " .. | |
| | Portable Magazine. | | | | |
| Mount Arrivé | Battery ...... 13 pr. Guns ...... 3 | | 3 | — " | |
| | Temporary Store. | | | | |
| Sallerie | Battery ...... { 18 pr. Guns ...... 4 | | 4 | | |
| | { 68 pr. Carrᵈ. 1 | | | | |
| Fort Amherst | Battery ...... 24 pr. Guns ...... 2 | | 2 | 19 " .. | |
| | Permanent Magazine. | | | | |
| South Pier | Battery ...... 9 pr. Guns ...... 2 | | 2 | " — | |
| | Temporary Store. | | | | |
| Hougue Fougue, centre of the Island | Battery ...... 18 pr. Gun ...... 1 | | 1 | — " — | |
| | For Signals of Alarm. | | | | |
| | Temporary Store in a Farm House. | | | | |

[GREENSLADE, PRINTER, GUERNSEY.]

OFFICE OF ORDNANCE,
Guernsey, 31 October 1816

Report of the monthly inspection of guns, 31st October, 1816, Guernsey.

P.R.O. WO 44/73

# Gun Specifications

| Calibre | Length of Piece | Length of Bore | Weight of Gun | Charge of Powder | Extreme range at 10° Elevation |
|---------|-----------------|----------------|---------------|------------------|-------------------------------|
| 24 pr | 9 ft 6 ins | 8 ft 11 ins | 50 cwt | 8 - 4 lb | 2870 - 2513 yds |
|  | 8 ft | 7 ft 5.5 ins | 40 cwt | 8 - 4 lb | 2870 - 2513 yds |
| 20 pr | 8 ft | 7 ft 6 ins | 37 cwt | 8 - 4 lb | 2660 - 1800 yds |
| 18 pr | 6 ft | 5 ft 6 ins | 27 cwt | 6 - 4 lb | 2668 - 2562 yds |
| 12 pr | 9 ft | 8 ft 6 ins | 34 cwt | 3.5 lb | 1800 yds at 60° elevation |
| 9 pr | 9 ft | 8 ft 6 ins | 31 cwt | 3.5 lb | 1800 yds at 60° elevation |
| 6 pr | 4 ft 6 ins | 4 ft | 5 cwt | 1.5 lb | 1200 yds at 5° elevation |

## CONVERSION CHART

| | | | |
|---|---|---|---|
| (lbs) | 1 Pound | = | 0.45 Kilograms |
| (cwt) | 1 Hundredweight | = | 50.8 Kilograms |
| (ins) | 1 Inch | = | 2.5 Centimetres |
| (ft) | 1 Foot | = | 30.5 Centimetres |
| (yds) | 1 Yard | = | 91 Centimetres |
| | 1 Mile | = | 1.6 Kilometres |

# Martello
# Tower

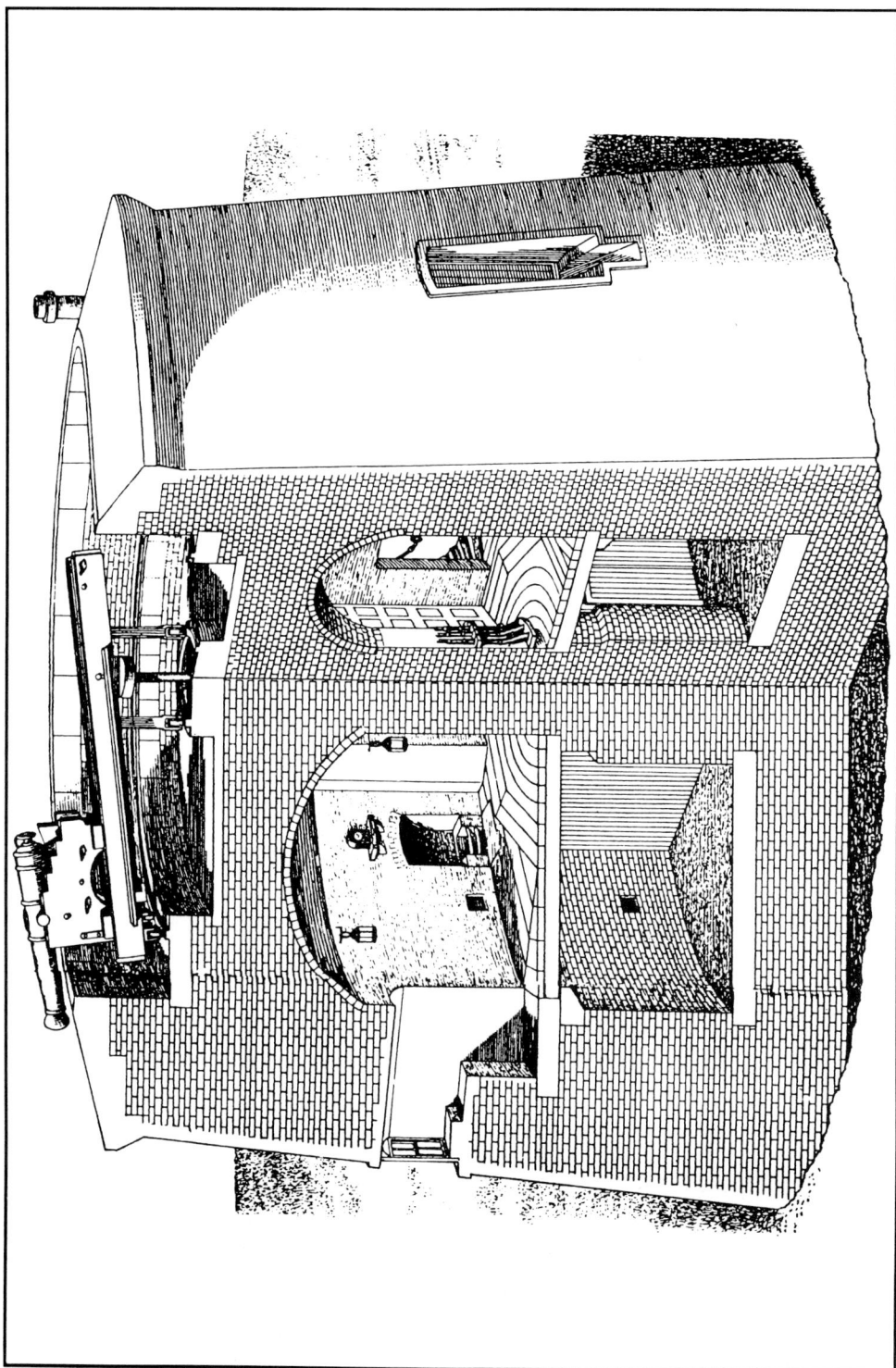

Martello Tower, taken from
History of Fortifications.

*Copyright: Macdonald/Orbis.*

# Appendix

Fort Grey now used as a Maritime Museum.

Tower 2, 1958.

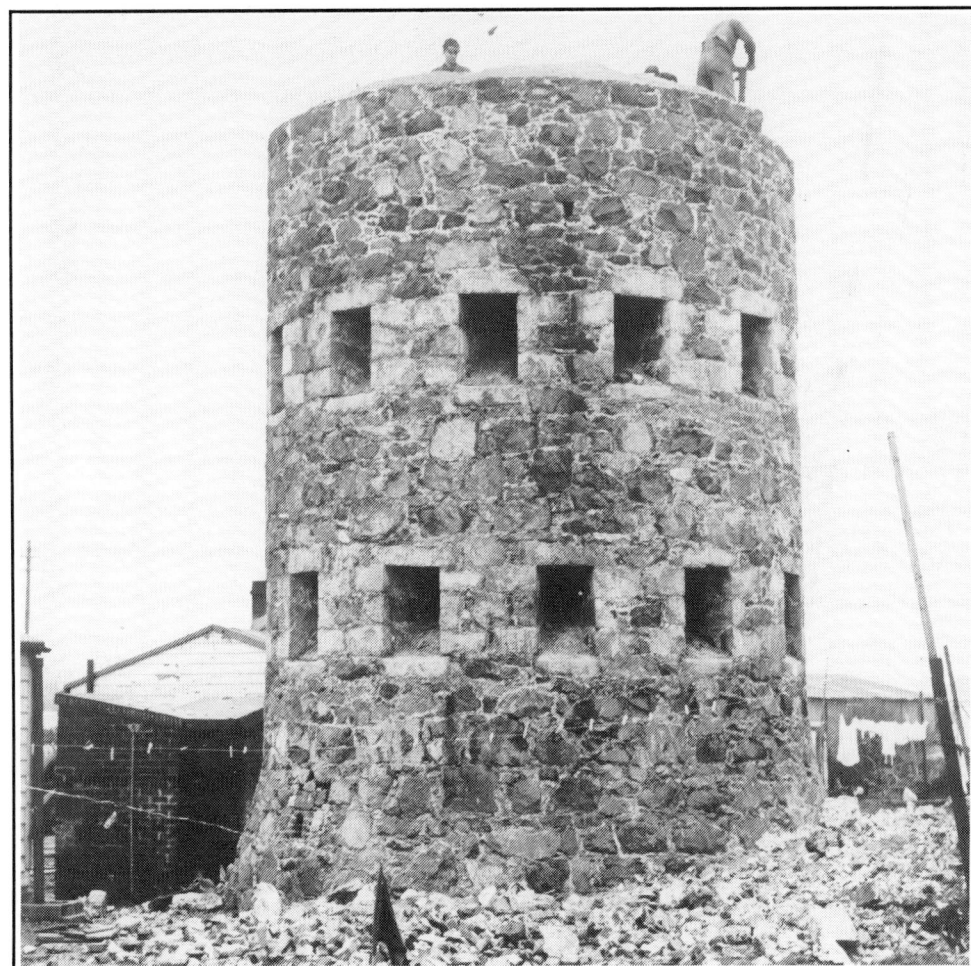

## Footnote:

*The Guernsey Martello Towers: Houmet, Saumarez and Fort Grey are all well protected and will stand as a testiment to those Napoleonic days when the threat of invasion from France seemed imminant.*

*The early pre-Martello Towers have their place in history as part of the development of coastal towers which in fact were the first to be built in the British Isles. Over the last 300 years three of the original fifteen towers have been demolished. The twelve remaining pre-martello towers although protected, are left uncared for.*

# Chronological Table of Events in the Channel Islands

**1066**    William, Duke of Normandy conquers England. Isles de Normandie *(Channel Islands)* become linked with the English Crown.

**1338**    French succeed in capturing Castle Cornet and occupying it for five years *(Guernsey)*.

**1356-7**    Island and Castle Cornet captured by the French and held for a few months *(Guernsey)*.

**1678-1680**    Charles II commissioned a Military Survey of the Channel Islands by Colonel George Legge.

**1778**    *(20th May)*. General Conway (Governor of Jersey) suggests the use of towers as a means of defending the islands. In the Autumn construction of pre-martello towers commenced in both Guernsey and Jersey.

**1779**    *(1st May)*. The French attempt a landing at St. Ouen's, Jersey.

**1780**    Guernsey Militia wear the red uniform for the first time.

**1780**    Fort Subscription, later renamed Fort Amherst was built at Paris Street *(Guernsey)*, through subscriptions from businessmen.

**1781**    *(5th January)*. French forces land at La Rocque *(Jersey)* and march to St. Helier.

**1782-1812**    Building of Fort George, Guernsey.

**1787**    An accurate Survey Map of Guernsey was produced by William Gardner. This was instigated by the Duke of Richmond, Master General of Ordnance.

**1789**    Sunday Militia Parades were abolished due to strong Methodist opposition *(Guernsey)*.

**1793**    *(Feb. 1st)*. War between France and England begins.

| | |
|---|---|
| **1794** | Naval engagement with a round tower at Mortella Point, Corsica. |
| **1802** | Peace of Amiens signed. |
| **1803** | Hostilities between France and England resumed. |
| **1803-1816** | Lieutenant General Sir John Doyle, Baronet, G.C.B., K.C., was Governor of Guernsey. |
| **1804** | Three Martello towers were constructed on the west coast of Guernsey. |
| **1805-12** | Martello towers built along the South coast of England. |
| **1806** | Draining of Braye du Valle commenced *(Guernsey)*. |
| **1807** | Building of Military Roads commenced *(Guernsey)*. |
| **1808** | Martello Towers built along the East coast of England. |
| **1811-1837** | Later Martello Towers built in Jersey. |
| **1815** | Battle of Waterloo. Napoleon finally defeated. |
| **1831** | Island Militia designated "Royal" by William IV *(Guernsey)*. |
| **1847** | Construction of Naval Base and Forts in Alderney. |
| **1854-6** | Construction of Brehon Tower *(Situated in Little Russel between Guernsey and Herm)*. |
| **1856** | Privateering abolished. |
| **1905** | Tower No. 2 demolished to make way for road-widening and tramsheds *(Guernsey)*. |
| **1941(?)** | Tower No. 8 demolished by the German occupying forces *(Guernsey)*. |
| **1958** | Tower No. 3 demolished by States of Guernsey for block of flats *(Guernsey)*. |

# Chronological Table of Events in the Channel Islands

# Pre-Martello Coastal Towers

| | |
|---|---|
| *20th May, 1778* | General Henry Seymour Conway (Governor of Jersey) wrote to Lord Weymouth, Secretary of State, proposing the construction of thirty coastal towers for the defence of Jersey. *(WO 46/10)* |
| *13th June, 1778* | Lord Weymouth passed an extract of Conway's letter to Lord Amherst, Master-General of the Ordnance, asking for an estimate of cost. *(WO 46/10)* |
| *3rd July, 1778* | Board of Ordnance informed Lord Weymouth that the cost would be £156 per tower. *(WO 55/372)* |
| *5th July, 1778* | Lord Weymouth signified 'the king's pleasure for thirty towers' to be erected in Jersey at a cost of £4,680. *(WO 55/372)* |
| *17th July, 1778* | Lord Weymouth signified the king's pleasure for fifteen towers to be erected in Guernsey " . . . of the same form and made as those ordered for the Island of Jersey". *(WO 55/372)* |
| *22nd July, 1778* | Board of Ordnance ordered Captain Basset (in transcript) proceed with erecting fifteen towers. *(WO 74/92) (Guernsey)* |
| *31st Aug., 1778* | *Diary.* Nicholas De Garis (Procureur des Pauvres of the Forest Parish) " . . . detailed account of the building of the Martello Tower at Petit Bôt." He gave the names of workmen together with wages" . . . forty men were employed, and the aggregate amounted to 1,239 days . . . the cost of the construction of the Tower being 1,339 livres tournois, or about £100 sterling." *(Société Guernesiaise).* |
| *30th Sept., 1778* | Actes des Etats "to acquire three pieces of Land, at States expense, requested by the said Lieut-Governor, on which to build three towers which His Majesty the King has ordered, with others, to be built at His government expense for the defence of the Island." *(Guernsey)* |
| *1789* | *Duke of Richmond Map.* By this date all of the fifteen towers were built in Guernsey but not of the same form and mode as those constructed in Jersey. |
| *6th Sept., 1787* | Office of Ordnance Towers. *(Guernsey).* Royal Engineers Report: " . . . smallness of their diameter, the fire from the Creneaux and even from the top is very inconsiderable . . . We approve of Towers, but would recommend a different construction." *(WO 55/808)* |
| *24th Sept., 1805* | In a letter to Lt. General Morse from Lt. Col. Mackelcan (Royal Engineers) referring to the building of the later towers on the west coast, a section of the letter comments " . . . . . The fifteen towers . . . were originally erected I believe by the Ordnance in General Conway's time." *(WO 55/5367) (Guernsey).* |

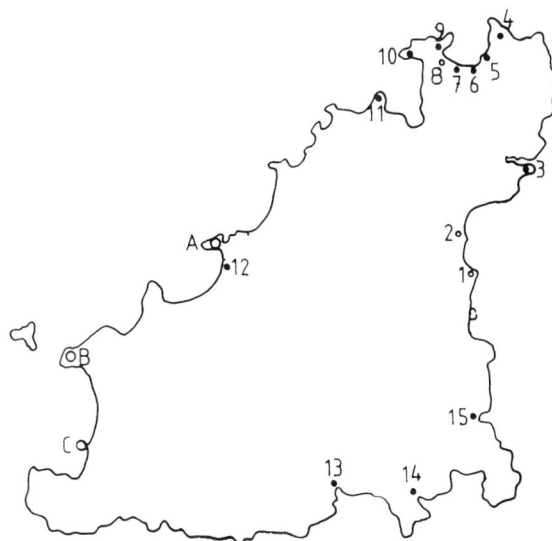

# PRE-MARTELLO TOWERS

| Tower Name | Date Built | *Still Standing |
|---|---|---|
| HOUGUE A LA PERRE  No. 1 | – | Destroyed in 1905 for tram shed and road widening. |
| HOUGUE LA PERE (Belle Greve) No. 2 | – | Destroyed 1958 for States Flats |
| MONT CREVELT (St. Sampson) No. 3 | – | * |
| TOWER No. 4 (near Fort Le Marchant) | – | * |
| TOWER No. 5 (Nid de l'Herbe) | – | * |
| TOWER No. 6 (L'Ancresse) | – | * |
| TOWER No. 7 (L'Ancresse) | – | * |
| TOWER No. 8 (nr. Golf Club) | – | Destroyed by Germans in World War II |
| TOWER No. 9 (Pembroke) | – | * |
| TOWER No. 10 (Chouet) | – | * |
| TOWER No. 11 (Rousse) | – | * |
| TOWER No. 12 (Vazon) | – | * |
| TOWER No. 13 (Petit Bôt) | 1778 | * |
| TOWER No. 14 (Saints Bay) | – | * |
| TOWER No. 15 (Fermain) | – | * |

## MARTELLO TOWERS WEST COAST - (NORTH TO SOUTH)

| | | |
|---|---|---|
| A.   FORT HOUMET | 1804 | * |
| B.   FORT SAUMAREZ | 1804 | German tower added during Occupation in World War II |
| C.   FORT GREY | 1804 | * |

# Guernsey Towers

*N.B. Numbering of towers differs on various plans and reports.*

# Bibliography

| | |
|---|---|
| MARTELLO TOWERS | Sheila Sutcliffe 1972 |
| HISTORY OF FORTIFICATIONS | Ian Hogg 1977 |
| HISTORY OF GUERNSEY | Berry 1815 |
| SURVEY OF THE CHANNEL ISLANDS | Colonel Legge 1680 |
| JERSEY MARTELLO TOWERS | |
|     SOCIETE JERSIAISE | H. R. S. Pocock 1971 |
| STRONGHOLD A HISTORY | |
|     OF MILITARY HISTORY | Martin B. Brice 1980 |
| THE CONSTITUTION AND LAW OF GUERNSEY | Sir John Loveridge 1975 |
| GUERNSEY 1066-1966 VOL. XXII No. 2 | The Guernsey Society's Quarterly review |
| A PICTORIAL HISTORY OF GUERNSEY | G. Stevens Cox 1979 |
| GUERNSEY ILLUSTRATED | 1900 |
| SOCIETE GUERNESIAISE VOL. XXI Pt. 2 | |
| A SHORT HISTORY OF THE TOWN OF | |
|     ST. SAMPSON | Victor Coysh 1985 |
| THE CHANNEL ISLANDS | Edith F. Carey 1930 |
| A HISTORY OF THE BAILIWICK OF GUERNSEY | L. James Marr 1982 |
| HISTORY OF THE CHANNEL ISLANDS | Raoul Lempriere 1974 |
| GUERNSEY AS IT WAS | Nick Machon 1985 |
| GUERNSEY PRESENT AND PAST | Ralph Durand 1933 |
| A HISTORICAL LOOK AT GUERNSEY | |
|     AND THE BAILIWICK | G. H. Mahy |
| THE BAILIWICK OF GUERNSEY | C. P. Le Huray 1952 |
| SEA-LIFE IN NELSON'S TIME | John Masefield 1972 |
| MILITARY UNIFORMS | 1973 |
| A SHORT HISTORY OF GUERNSEY | P. J. Johnson |
| ACTES DES ETATS VOLS, I, II, III, IV, V. | |
| GUERNSEY THROUGH THE LENS | Victor Coysh and Carel Toms 1978 |
| GUERNSEY THROUGH THE LENS AGAIN | Victor Coysh and Carel Toms 1982 |
| ROYAL GUERNSEY | Victor Coysh 1977 |
| BAILIWICK BASTIONS | L. James Marr 1985 |
| GUERNSEY MONTH ILLUSTRATED MAGAZINE | 1873 |
| GUERNSEY NEWSPAPERS | |
| EPIC SEA BATTLES | William Koetling |
| GREAT SEA BATTLES | Oliver Warner |
| A HISTORY OF ARTILLERY | Ian V. Hogg 1974 |
| THE HISTORY OF FORTIFICATION | Ian Hogg 1981 |

# Glossary of Military Terms

BANQUETT: Raised area inside tower where the traversing wheel runs.

BARBETTE: Firing step on parapet.

BULWARK: Rampart, earthwork.

CAPONIER: Covered passage across ditch of fort.

CARRONADE: Short large calibred muzzel-loading cannon designed by General Robert Melville. First cast by the Carron Iron Company, Stirlingshire, Scotland in 1776. Range 500 yards.

CHAUSSE: A timber boom placed across harbour.

CRENEAUX: Loopholes to fire muskets from.

CULVERIN: A cannon 5.5 in. firing 18 lb shot.

DEMI-CULVERIN: Cannon of 4.5 inch bore.

EMBRAZURES: Opening in parapet for gun.

FALCON: An ancient kind of cannon. 2.5 in. firing 2.5 lb shot.

GLACIS: Bank sloping down from fort, on which attackers are exposed to fire.

MACHICOULES: Opening in parapet to be able to fire down the side of the wall.

MERLONS: The part between two embrazures.

MINION: A small kind of ordnance of about 3 inches calibre.

PARAPET: A bank or earth or a wall over which a soldier may fire.

RAVELIN: Fortification - outwork of two faces, forming salient angle outside main ditch before curtain.

REBOUBT: A detached outwork with no flanking defence.

SAKER: A small variant of the Demi-culverin.

# Illustrations, Sketches and Photographs

Braye du Valle *(Guernsey), Société Guernesiaise Map, Major S.C. Curtis*    40
Brehon Tower *(Guernsey), Photograph: Brian Green*    53
Brickfield *(Best's in Guernsey), Photograph: E.B. Best*    72

Castle Cornet *(Guernsey), Museum Education Service Plans*    54
                *Photograph: Brian Green*    55
Channel Islands Map    6
Comparison Chart, *Comparing Specification of Towers*    50
Forts: *(Guernsey)*
         George Gateway, *Sketch*    55
         Grey,    *Plan 28, Sketch 29, Plans 66*
            *Photograph: Brian Green 69, Photograph: Victor Coysh 87*
         Houmet,    *Photograph: Brian Green 32, Plans 62*
            *Photograph: Brian Duquemin 68*
         Mont Crevelt,    *Plans 58, Photograph: Brian Green 59*
         Pembroke, *Plan*    52
         Saumarez,    *Plans 38, Photograph: Victor Coysh 64*
            *Photograph: Eric Grimsley 65, Photograph: Adrian Miller 68*
Geological Map *(Guernsey), Map, Société Guernesiaise*    70
Guernsey Map,    6,7
         Position of Alarm Gun    9
         Position of Martello Towers    21
         1802 Map    26 & 27
         Doyle Map 1803    30 & 31
         Martello Towers    33
         All Coastal Towers    91
Guernsey Militia Uniforms, *Guernsey Philatelic Bureau*    8,73
Guns, *Drill SBML Coastal Guns, Photographs: Royal Artillery Institution*    74
         Gun Platform, (Jersey Plans)    78
         Reports 1801    79,80
         Reports 1816    81-84
         Specification Chart    85
         Smasher (Carronade), *sketch*    77
         Traversing Frame    76
Jersey Map, *Showing Coastal Towers*    44
Loopholes, *Sketch*    15
Machicoule, *Sketch*    47
Martella Tower *(Corsica), Section*    12
Martello Towers    *(England)* South & East Coast Map    16
         Eastbourne *(Wish Tower), Section*    14
         Hythe No. 13 *(Kent), Section*    13
         Nr. Hythe, *King and His Army and Navy News*    51
         Pevensey Bay, *Illustrated London News 1889*    15
         Martello Tower, *Showing gun platform, Macdonald/Orbis*    86
         Rochester Conference, *Original Sketch*    14
Martello Towers    *(Guernsey)*
         Critical Report    34
         Directive to Inspect Towers    36
         Request to Fit Out Towers    34
Martello Towers    *(Jersey)*
         Kempt, *Plan and Section*    42
         Lewis, *Plan and Section*    42
         Noirmont, *Section*    43
Pre-Martello Towers *(Guernsey),*    *Section 17, Plans 24, Plan 46*
         Building Details *(Petit Bôt, Guernsey)*    20,22,23
         Hougue à la Perre,    *Plan 56, Photograph: Victor Coysh 56,87*
            *Photograph: Brian Duquemin 57*
         L'Ancresse No. 6, *Photograph: Martin Walsh*    63
         Petit Bôt Tower No. 13, *Photograph: Bernard Hassell*    19
         Rousse Tower No. 11,    *Photograph: Brian Green 40, Plan 60*
            *Photograph: Martin Walsh 63*
         Saints No. 14, *Photograph: Martin Walsh*    25
         Vazon No. 12,    *Plan 61, Photograph: Adrian Miller 63*
Pre-Martello Towers *(Jersey),*    *Section 17, Tower No. 3 Print 18, Section 43*
            *Plan 46, Plans 48*
Privateering,    Details    10
         Letter of Marque    11

# Concise Index A-I

Alarm gun 9
Alderney Martello Towers *(not built)* 53
American War of Independence
    (1776) 3,17,75
Amherst, Lord, Master General of
    the Ordnance 17
ARMAMENT:
*Col. Legge Report 1680 (Guernsey)*
    73,75
*Gun Platform Jersey* 78
*Gun Reports & Inspec. 1801* 79,80
*Gun Reports & Inspec. 1816* 81-84
*Gun Specification* 85
*Gun Names* 93
*Mont Crevelt* 59

Bassett, Capt. 15,19,21,25,47
Braye du Valle 39,40,41
Brehon Tower 53
Bricks & Brickmaking 70,71
Building Materials *(Granite)* 71

Castle Cornet 7,54,55
Castle, Vale *See Vale Castle*
Carronades 49,51,75,77,78
Channel Island Map 6
Chateau de Rocquaine *See Fort Grey*
Chronological Table of
    Channel Island Events 88,89
Clameur de Haro 21
Comparison Chart
    *(Martello and Pre-Martello)* 50
Conway, Gov. of Jersey 13,17,43,75
Conversion Chart *(Imp.- Metric)* 85

De Garis, Diary 19,20,22,23
De Garis, Journal 19,71
De Preaux, Peter 8
Don, Lt. Gov. Gen. *(Jersey)* 29
Doyle, Lt. Gov. Gen.
    *(Guernsey)* 5,29,33,35,37,39,41
    47,49,59,67,69,75
Duchy of Normandy 7
Duke of Normandy 7

Ford, Captain 15
FORTS: *(Guernsey)*
*Amherst* 11
*George* 55
*Grey* 28,29,33,35,37,50,51,63,66
    67,69,87
*Hougue á la Perre* 56,57
*Houmet* 32,33,37,50,51,62,63,68
*Mont Crevelt* 33,57
*Ownership (Guernsey) 1847* 11
*Pembroke* 52
*Saumarez (L'Ereé)* 29,33,37,38,49,50
    64,65,67,68
Fort Subscription 11
French *(Occupation of C.I.)* 7
    Jersey Invasions 1779 9
                1781 9
Furnaces 33

Gray, Andrew *(Military Draftsman)* 33,35
Grey, Fort *See Forts*
Guernsey *(Bailiwick)* 7
Guernsey Geological Map 70
Guernsey Map 1802 26,27
            1803 30,31
Guernsey Martello Towers 29,31-39,
    49,50,51
Guernsey Militia 8,9,73
Guernsey Pre-Martello Towers 13
    18-25,47,49,50,59,63,81,90,91
Guns: *See Armament*
*Drill* 74
*Specification* 85
*Names* 93

Henry, Thomas *(Builder)* 33,35,41
Houmet *See Forts*
Humphrey, Major John, R.E. 29,77

Inspection of Martello Towers
    *(Guernsey)* 36,37
Irving, Lt. Gen. Col.
    Paulus Aemilius 9

# Concise Index J-Z

JERSEY:
*Invasion 1779*                                        9
        *1781*                                        9
*Map Showing*
        *position of Towers*        44,45
*Martello Towers*
        *1807-1814*            43,44-47,49,51
        *1835*                42,43,44,45,51
*Pre-Martello Towers*    13,15,43,47-49
John, King                                            8
**K**empt                *See Jersey Towers*
Kilns, *(Guernsey)*                        71
**L**and Reclamation *(Guernsey)*
                *See Braye du Valle*
La Rocco *(Jersey)*                        43
Legge Report (Col. George Legge)
1680 Military Survey  7,9,39,67,73,75
Le Guet *(Guernsey)*                    53
L'Érée, Fort Saumarez        *See Forts*
L'Etac                *See Jersey Towers*
Lewis Tower        *See Jersey Towers*
**M**acarty, Gov. Charles              7
Machicoules                        18,43,47
Mackelcan, Lieut Col. Comm. R.E.
                        29,33,35,39,47,49
Mont Crevelt                *See Forts*
Mortella Point                        12,13
Martello Towers:
*England. S. & E. Coast*        15,16,50
*Guernsey*                *See Guernsey*
*Jersey*                        *See Jersey*
Military Roads *(Guernsey)*            41
Militia        *See Guernsey Militia*
Morse, Lieut. *(Inspector General)*    35
**N**apoleon                                15
Noirmont                *See Jersey Towers*
Normandy,        *Duchy & Duke See D.*
**P**atois *(Guernsey)*                        7
Pembroke Tower *(Guernsey)*          53

Penalty for defective building
    (Thomas Henry Junior)            33
Petit Bôt Tower *(Guernsey)*
    Building details            20,22,23
Pre-Martello Towers *(Guernsey)*
    Map Plan, 13,17,19,21,24,47,56,57
                    58-61,87,90,91
Pre-Martello Towers *(Jersey)*
                        17,18,43-48
**R**eports:
*1787 on Guernsey*                    25
*1802 (Guernsey) John Humphrey*    29
*1803 (Guernsey) Lieut. Col.*
    *Mackelcan* 29,39,49,57,63,67
*1803 (Guernsey) Lieut. Gov. Maj.*
    *Gen. Sir John Doyle*        29,67
Report on Ordnance *(State of)*
                *See Armament*
Report on Martello Towers *(Guernsey)*
*Critical*                            32,37
*Official*                            36,37
Richmond, Duke of                    21
Rocquaine Castle, Fort Grey  *See Forts*
Rousse Battery *(Guernsey)*        60,63
Royal Engineers *(Committee)*        15

**S**aumarez Fort                *See Forts*
Saumarez, Rear Adml. Sir James 33,39
Saxe, Marshall                        17
Seigneurs                                7
St. Sampson Harbour                39
Sussex Tower        *See Alderney Towers*
**T**owers: Brehon                        53
Towers  *See Martello*
        *England, Guernsey and Jersey*
Traversing Frame *(Guernsey)*        76,77
**V**ale Castle                                7
Vazon Battery                        60,63
Vicomtes *(Feudal System)*            7
**W**eymouth, Lord                    17,19
Wicks, Major, Commander of Artillery
    *(Guernsey)*                        35